T0197180

JOB'S
OTHER LIFE

JOB'S
OTHER LIFE

Beyond Suffering to Restoration

John Schuch

WESTBOW
P R E S S®
A DIVISION OF THOMAS NELSON
& ZONDERVAN

WestBow Press books may be ordered through booksellers or by contacting:

WestBow Press
A Division of Thomas Nelson & Zondervan
1663 Liberty Drive
Bloomington, IN 47403
www.westbowpress.com
1 (866) 928-1240

ISBN: 978-1-9736-6522-9 (sc)
ISBN: 978-1-9736-6521-2 (e)

Print information available on the last page.

WestBow Press rev. date: 10/28/2019

CONTENTS

INTRODUCTION

There are two reasons why I am writing on the life of Job. First, this book became alive to me in my early days as a believer and since then God has led me to go back and meditate on Job's life. Second, I hear the same question over and over from believers, "Why do the Godly suffer?". It just seems believers refer to Job's suffering and hardly ever speak of Satan's attacks or how Job was restored. Believers refer to Job but know very little of his complete life.

It was in Bible College in summer school that I had to take a course called Hebrew History and my professor was Fred Afman. That particular day he went through the life of Job and his encounters with his three friends and the results of Job's life. I can hardly remember all that was said, but God's Word gripped my heart and I had a new appreciation for the man, Job. I continued to go back to his life ; meditating on it. I knew there was more to the life of Job than what was being spoken by most believers concerning Job. It seemed I heard people refer to Job's life, but hardly ever heard anyone teach on the book of Job from beginning of his life to the end.

I kept going back over his life and wrote down what God was revealing to me. Then in South Shields, England, a fellow elder gave me a very small book on the life of Job. The author's name was E. Walker and I have never seen his book since then. What was so inspiring was his teaching on Satan's encounter with God and his attack on Job. This gave me greater revelation on Job and I found that the rest of Scripture was in agreement with what God was revealing to me.

Since then I have taught on the life of Job and I keep meditating on his life letting God feed my spirit. God has revealed so many things to me. How Satan was able to attack Job and his being restored is hardly mentioned speaking of Job. Many believers never realize there was a fourth man who spoke to Job. In fact, many believers brush him aside with the other three. Bible teachers and believers seem to spend more time on Job's suffering than on his restoration. I believe this is Satan's deception. If Satan can't get us away from the Lord, then he has us focus more on our trials, difficulties, and hardships than on what God can and wants to do in our lives.

The second reason I am writing on Job is the misunderstanding of the events in his life. This affects our faith because when things happen to us, we go back to Job's life and say, "Well, it happened to Job and it is God's will for this to happen to me." Then we hear all kinds of teaching on why the godly suffer. The question we ought to be asking is "**How was Satan able to attack a man who had God's protection?**"

What is God's purpose and intention in giving us the revelation of the life of Job? Is it to teach us that all the bad things that happen to us is God's will? God is all knowing and all powerful, so He must allow it. Yet we miss that Satan brought the curse into the world and he operates the curse. To attribute God with the curse of sin upon the life of a believer is in total contradiction to God's redemptive purpose for man. Galatians 3:13-14—"Christ redeemed us from the curse of the law by becoming a curse for us." Praise God! He didn't want the work of the evil one, the curse, to operate in Job's life, nor in any believer's life. God's revelation of the life of Job is not to teach us that defeat and disasters in our lives are the will of our Father, but **the work of the evil one and how we can have victory over him.**

Listed below are the experiences of Job's life. We will see what is said about each of them. This will give us a greater revelation in understanding things that we may experience and how we can respond to them in gaining the victory over the evil one.

> Job was a very Godly man.
> Job had God's protection.
> Job encountered Satan's attacks.
> Job was given faulty counsel.
> Job tried to defend and justify himself.
> Job was given counsel that would lead to his restoration.
> Job's eyes were finally turned off himself and onto God.

Job heard the Word of God.

Job repented.

Job prays for his three friends.

Job was restored with twice as much as before.

CHAPTER 1

God's Purpose for
Man in Creation

As we approach the life of Job, right away we are brought face to face with God's encounter with Satan. It is easy to see things just in the natural, earthly realm and not realize what is taking place in the spirit realm of evil forces and Godly forces. If we do not have an understanding of these two forces, then it will be difficult to understand what God is saying to us in the life of Job. It is through men like Job that God has so much to teach us. It is important to realize these two forces or kingdoms are still active today.

Satan's kingdom is called the kingdom of darkness or the kingdom of this world. How was Satan's kingdom established on this earth and what power and influence does it have on mankind? What is meant by God's kingdom? Where is it in operation and what influence does it have over man? Both these forces had a powerful influence on Job. These two forces or kingdoms have an influence on our lives and as believers we want to know how we can live under God's reign instead of Satan's.

The answers to these questions begin with God at His creation of man. It is so vital for believers to understand God's purpose in His creation of man. Often our failure to understand God's purpose in creation leads us to a misunderstanding of what caused these events to take place in Job's life. If we do not see clearly the events in Job's life and how they came about, then how can we understand the things that happen to us? Let's begin with God in the beginning.

In God's creation of man, we find three basic things God gave to man. I call them God's creation purpose.

GOD'S CREATION PURPOSE
1. His image—God's life.
2. His dominion—God's authority.
3. His blessings—God's resources.

God's purpose will never change. That is why believers from the time of Adam up through Jesus and His church find these three things are to be active in their lives. Believers before Jesus and after Jesus often failed to live in the power of these provisions. Yet Jesus is our prime example of these things being fulfilled in His life. Let's examine the three creation purposes.

His Image

God created man in His own image. Genesis 1:26-27—"Then God said, 'Let us make man in our image, according to our likeness'...so God created man in His own image, in the image of God He created him; male and female."

The Hebrew words for *image* and *likeness* mean nature, copy, characteristics, and essence. In other words, Adam was created in the likeness of God's life. Many Rabbis and Jewish scholars interpret this to mean that God created man an 'intelligent, speaking species'. This set man apart from all other created things. Even in His creation He spoke things into existence. Like God, man is a conscious, speaking person.

Another major image of God's creation in man was that he was created in love. Jesus testified to this in His words, "Father' you loved me before the creation of the world." Love was active with God before the creation. That is why Scripture says, "God is love." Man was created in this same image of love: to receive love, to live in love, and to give love.

His Dominion

God gave complete dominion of the earth to man. Genesis 1:26 and 28—"Let them have dominion over the fish of the sea and the birds of the air, and over the cattle, over all the earth and over every creeping thing that creeps on the earth. ...fill the earth and subdue it, have dominion over the fish of the sea, the birds of the air and over every living thing that moves on the earth." In the Authorized Version, the word *dominion* is used. To rule or have dominion means reign, kingly rule. The Lord said to 'subdue', which means to bring it under control. Did the Lord intend for Adam to spread the garden of Eden throughout the earth? Is this what is meant by being fruitful and multiplying throughout the earth? These words reveal man being given authority from the Lord to reign on the earth.

In other words, God put the whole earth under man's control. This was God's purpose and mandate that man had full responsibility of the whole earth. Psalm 8:5-8— "You made him (man) a little lower than the angels and You have crowned him with glory and honor. You made him to have dominion over the works of Your hands. You have put all things under His feet. All sheep and oxen, even the beast of the field, the birds of the air and the fish of the sea." Psalm 115:16 "The heaven, even the heavens, are the Lord's: but the earth He has given to the children of men." God did not give man the ownership of the earth, but He did entrust complete rule of it unto man. Man with God's life and resources was to be God's representative on the earth. In the very beginning, God delegated the earth to Adam (man) to rule, manage, and govern.

The beautiful fact about man being ruler over the earth is that Adam was related to God and he was God's representative on the earth. All that God would do on the earth would always be through man. Man would always be God's link to His activity on the earth. Adam was given the responsibility of the garden; it was completely in his care. Even the naming of the animals was in Adam's complete control. God did not try to step in and help him. Once God spoke His Word that the earth was under man's control and management, then God will not change nor alter what He has already spoken.

> "Adam represented God, presenting again His will on the earth. Adam was God's governor or manager here. The earth was Adam's assignment—it was under Adam's charge or care. Adam was the watchman or guardian. How things went on planet earth, for better or worse, depended on Adam and his offspring. Please think about that. If the earth remained a paradise, it would be because of humankind. If things became messed up, it would be because of humankind. If the serpent ever gained control, it would be because of humankind. Humanity really was in charge." Dutch Sheets: Intercessory Prayer 1996 copyright Bethany House Publishers

His Blessing

The third thing God did for man was to bless him. Genesis1:28—"God blessed them." Verse 29-30 we read that God gave them seeds. Anything they needed was given to them by God. God's blessing meant that God was man's complete source. All that Adam would ever need would be fulfilled by the Lord. God was extending His invisible realm to the visible and God would supply all that man needed. All the resources that Adam would need would be given to him by God.

All three of these creation purposes was fulfilled in our Lord Jesus Christ as man.

1. Image. Jesus came in the full image of His Father. His life reveals to us God's image can be manifested in a life on this earth. Jesus was the 'express image of His Father.' Hebrews.1:3 (NKJV) All the Father's fullness was in Jesus. Colossians. 1:9, 2:19

2. Dominion. Jesus had complete dominion on this earth. He had dominion over natural events, stilling the water, controlling the winds, walking on the water. His dominion was over Satan and his demons. He took authority over all sickness. He was His Father's representative on this earth and Jesus knew He was given this authority.

3. Blessing. Jesus trusted His Father for all His resources. He was able to feed over five thousand with just five small loaves and two small fish. His Father's resource provided for His disciples to fill two boats of fish after fishing all night and catching nothing. Satan tempted Jesus to change stones into bread which would mean trusting Satan as His resource; however, He knew His Father was His complete source.

CHAPTER 2

What Took Place
When Man Sinned

In Genesis chapter 3, we read of Adam's sin. We know that sin is doing wrong and falling short of God's goodness and glory. Yet, the act of sin goes far deeper than just doing wrong; it always means submitting to Satan. Satan's goal in tempting Adam and Eve was to have them submit to him and be independent of God. Sin always means we obey Satan instead of God. Once Adam and Eve sinned, they died to God and obeyed Satan, and submitted to him.

The three things God gave to man at his creation are now under Satan's control. After man sinned he was still alive physically and mentally but he was dead in his relationship with the Lord. This means Adam's relationship to God is the death of his spirit man to God. That is why in the New Testament sin is always spoken of as death. Romans 6:23 (NKJV) "Wages of sin is death." Ephesians 2:1 (NKJV) "who were dead in your transgressions and sins." This death to God means that man being God's representative on the earth is destroyed. By Adam submitting unto Satan, he came under Satan's control. This means all things on earth are now under Satan's control. The complete dominion that was given to Adam now comes under Satan's control; for in sinning, Adam submitted his life to Satan. Man is now independent of God and he is now under Satan's control and curse. Satan has now usurped God's place of reigning through man and has brought creation under his control. Man under Satan's control cannot represent God on this earth. All that God placed in man is now under Satan's control. In this world, it has left God on the outside and Satan in control.

Now this raises a very serious question. If God is God, then He is all powerful and can do anything. How can He possible be on the outside? The question is not that God is not powerful and able to do all things for He is God. But He will never go against what He has spoken. His Word is His life and once He speaks it, He honors it. **The sovereignty of God will never over ride what God has spoken.** Once He speaks something, He is always true to His Word. An example of this is in Revelation 4–5. John was taken into heaven and John saw a scroll in the right hand of Him who sat upon the throne and it was sealed. The question was asked, who is worthy to open the seals and it says no one in heaven or earth was worthy to open the seals. Surely, God being God had the power to open this scroll. But because of His Word, He would not do it. His Word says Christ was slain from the creation of the world. In Revelation 13:8, we know that the Lamb of God was worthy to open the seals. God's power of being God Almighty never violates His Word, "upholding all things by the word of His power." Hebrews. 1:3 (NKJV)

Even on bumper stickers, I have seen signs that say, "God is in control." Many believers say, "God in His Sovereignty is in complete control". However, God's sovereignty never works apart from His Word. If He has spoken something, then God's sovereignty is under His Word. God's sovereignty is His Word; and His word is His sovereignty. God will never go against His Word. "For You have magnified Your Word above all your Name." Psalms 138:2b (NKJV) It was God's sovereignty that spoke the word putting man in control of the world. His sovereignty does not change. Therefore, what God has set in motion by His word will not change. God spoke His word, placing all rule and authority of the earth under man. It was man who yielded to the evil one and placed these things under Satan. Satan has gained control and we will see what Scripture says about Satan being the ruler of this world.

If we say this leaves God on the outside and Satan in control, then what hope is there for humanity? This is the glorious message of salvation. There is a way back to God being in control. God redeems man from Satan's control, bringing him back under His reign to once again be His representative on the earth. God's will is to restore man to his creation purpose. God honors His Word that man is to be His representative. Just because man sinned and submitted to the evil one does not give God the right to go against His word. This is why God redeeming man back to Himself is so powerful. Man comes back under God's creation purpose. This means the image, reign, and resources of God's life is restored to man.

Is God reigning or is Satan reigning? The answer is yes! Satan reigns in the world and its system. God reigns in His people. Abraham is an example of God reigning in His people. Abraham believed God and it was credited to him as righteousness. In other words, Abraham received God's life. This does not mean that God did not have believers before Abraham, such as Enoch, Noah, and others. But in Abraham, God was giving to us His revelation of salvation to man. In salvation, God is once again exercising His authority in the earth. Abraham is called the Father of faith and the father of all believers. His life is an example of one being under God's reign. This salvation was given to Abraham's son Isaac, and to his grandson, Jacob. Then through the nation Israel in Exodus 19:5–6 "then you shall be a special treasure to Me above all people...and you shall be to Me a Kingdom of priests and a holy nation." They were His kingdom people under His reign. They were His priests, which means they represent God on this earth. The good news is that man does not have to be under Satan's control. This is what salvation is all about. It seems that many evangelical believers emphasize that salvation is a ticket to heaven. Praise God! Salvation is our assurance of being with our Lord, but it is far more than just getting to heaven. It is living heaven's life on this earth. In the prayer Jesus taught His disciples to pray, Matthew 6:10 "Your Kingdom come. Your will be done on earth as in heaven." Jesus was teaching this prayer in the midst of this world being under Satan's control that God's reign can be established in His people.

It is important to realize that God put man in control of the earth and man by submitting to Satan gave this control over to Satan. This is why God could not take back control except through man. Jesus had to come to this earth as man. Just as man was given control and sin came through him, so must salvation come through a man. This means the only way God will regain is through man. In Genesis 3:15, we read that God will send one born of woman, a man, and He will crush Satan's head. It was needful that Jesus came as man.

CHAPTER 3

Jesus came to Establish God's Reign on the Earth

Jesus' announced the coming of His Kingdom on this earth. If God were in control of this world, why would Jesus announce His Kingdom Reign? If we do not understand the distinction between Satan's reign and God's reign, than we will confuse events that happen to us. In Jesus' time, they said His works were done by Satan. Today many believers give God the credit for what Satan has done. If we do not see this distinction, than we will not know who is behind events in our lives. Who was the source of Job's children being killed? Jesus went to the source when he said, "Satan (the thief) comes to kill, steal, and destroy." John 10:10 The following verses show Satan's control in this world and his reign.

II Corinthians 4:4—Satan is referred to as "the god of

this age." This is the same word god in Greek that refers to God—Theos.

I John 5:19—"We know that we are children of God, and the whole world lies under the sway of the wicked one." Note the distinction made between God's children and the rest of the world being under Satan's control.

Revelation 12:9—"The great dragon was cast down, that serpent of old called the devil and Satan, who deceives the whole world." Here it says "deceives the whole world". If Satan has the power to deceive, than he has control over those he is deceiving.

Three times in John's gospel, Jesus refers to Satan as "the ruler of this world." John 12:31; 14:30; and 16:11. The Greek word for ruler is 'archon'. It means to rule. It is used for Christ in Revelation 1:5 as King. Jesus testified of Satan's realm and authority in this world. In John 14:30 Jesus states this ruler has no hold on Him. This is a very powerful verse because it points out that although Satan is in control of the world, there is a realm where God's life and control have more authority and power than Satan's.

Satan was never in control of Jesus. Even His death on the cross was never under Satan's control. Jesus said concerning His life, "No one (Satan) takes if from me, but I lay it down of my own accord. I have authority to lay it down and authority to take it up again." John 10:18 Though Satan is the god of this world, God's people are not under his control and the only way he can control a believer is for that believer to submit to Satan instead of God. In Jesus' temptation in the wilderness, recorded in Luke

4:5-6; it says that Satan showed Jesus all the kingdoms of the world in a moment of time. Than Satan said to Jesus, "I will give you all their authority and splendor for it has been given to me and I can give it to anyone I want." Luke 4:6 Satan tempted Jesus with what was given to him and if Jesus would obey, He would have submitted to Satan just like the first Adam. Jesus never once submitted to Satan; therefore, He never came under Satan's control. This is why Jesus could say John 14:30 (NKJV)"for the ruler of this world is coming and he has nothing in me." John 14:30 says "He has not hold on me." Jesus was totally submitted to His Father. Jesus knew His battle was not just against people, but against Satan and his controlling power. This is why sin is not just doing wrong but yielding to the evil one. Never underestimate the power and control of Satan in this world nor doubt the reign of Jesus in our lives. His cross is greater the Adam's fall.

It is in Jesus' life that we see such a great distinction between Satan's kingdom or control and God's. Jesus and John the Baptist came announcing the Kingdom, or reign, of God on this earth. What was lost by man has now been regained in God's salvation of man. Christ came as man and gave to us God's salvation in His death and resurrection. It is through the salvation of man that God can now minister His life and reign in the earth. Have you noticed the words that speak of salvation: redeem, reconcile, renew, restoration, and revive? These words speak of God bringing man back under His reign. Man needs to be brought back to his original purpose. The glorious purpose in Salvation is to restore man back into God's image and under His reign. The moment one becomes a believer, that one is brought from Satan's kingdom reign into God's reign. Paul in Colossians 1:13 spoke of the two kingdoms. "For He has delivered us from the power (dominion) of darkness and conveyed us into the kingdom of the Son of His love." The word dominion in the Greek is 'exousia', which means authority. The same word is used in Matthew 9:6 (NKJV) "the Son of man has power (authority) on earth to forgive sins." This word "dominion" speaks of Satan's reign and it is just the opposite of God's reign. God's reign is a reign of light or life; and Satan's reign is a reign of darkness and death. What is needful to see is that there are two kingdoms. Two invisible forces at work. Those forces were active in Job's day and they are still active today.

The distinction in Scripture of Jesus teaching about the world and His life

The distinction between God's kingdom reign and Satan's is revealed to us in John's gospel. Notice how often Jesus uses the word "world" in contrast to His life and reign.

> John 8:23—"you are of this world; I am not of this world."

> John 9:5—"While I am in the world, I am the light of the world."

John 14:30—"For the prince of this world is coming, He has no hold on Me."

John 15:19—"If you were of the world, the world would love its own. Yet because you are not of the world, but I chose you out of the world, therefore the world hates you." (NKJV)

John 17:6—"I have manifested Your name to the men whom you have given Me out of th world."(NKJV)

John 17:14—"for they are not of the world, just as I am not of the world."

John 17:15—"My prayer is not that you take them out of the world, but that you protect them from the evil one."

John 17:16—"They are not of the world, even as I am not of the world."

John 17:18—"As you sent me into the world, I also have sent them into the world."

Ever since the fall and the salvation of man, these two forces have been at war. Job didn't realize all that was taking place in the heavenly realm. All he could see happening was in the natural, physical realm. Job didn't have all the revelation that we have today, the coming of Jesus, and the complete Word of God that reveals this great battle. Job's battle was not just in the natural realm, but what Scripture calls the heavenly realm. It was not just in the physical but the spirit realm of evil forces, that is, Satan and his demons against God.

In our study of Job, it is very important to understand what is from God and what is from Satan. This is why Scripture tells believers to "discern", which means to know right from wrong, Scriptural truth from error. It also means to discern Satan, his power, his ability, how he attacks lives, and the result of these attacks. In contrast, we are to discern what God has done through His people in both the Old Testament and the New Testament and what has been accomplished for us in Jesus. This discerning means to see what is of God and what is of Satan. The religious leaders during Jesus' ministry could not discern what was from God and what was from Satan. These leaders attributed Jesus' work to Satan. (See Matthew 12) They were so hard hearted that they were saying Jesus' ministry was from Satan. Their darkness was so great that they saw Jesus as the son of Satan instead of the Son of God. Today, many believers ascribe Satan's work to God. Satan can do all sorts of things to believers and many just sit back and say it is from God. Then, they use Job's life to prove it is from God or that God allows it.

Job experienced some very horrible things. Did God allow all of His children to be killed? What does God's Word say about all the bad things we experience? Are those things from Satan or from God? Did God even permit them to happen? Did Job give credit to God for what Satan did to him? These are important questions because believers refer to Job when they experience negative things in their lives. The world loves to blame God for all the bad things that happen. They say 'it is an act of God.' Yet believers come along and say God is allowing these things to teach me. Is that true? Does God use illness, accidents, or death to teach His followers? Did God permit these things to happen to Job to teach him? No! God does not use these things to teach us. God has given us His Word to teach us of His life. Only through His Word can we understand and discern Satan's reign and God's reign, to know what is from Satan's reign, and what we can expect from God's reign.

CHAPTER 4

What God says about Job

Most Bible scholars believe Job lived about the time of Abraham, probably before Abraham. One reason it seems that he lived during this time is the longevity of Job's life. Both Ezekiel (Old Testament) and James (New Testament) refer to Job. Job lived in Uz and the Bible says he was the greatest man in the East. He had 7 sons and 3 daughters. It says he owned 7,000 sheep, 3,000 camels, 500 yoke of oxen, 500 donkeys, and a large number of servants. If you have had any experience in farming, then you may realize how many people he would need to tend and feed that amount of stock. No wonder it says he was the greatest man in the East.

Not only was Job very wealthy, but God spoke very highly of him. God said, he was blameless and turned from evil. Job desired not to sin but to walk with God. He had a very deep trust in God. Living during this time, Job took his responsibility of sacrificing unto the Lord seriously. God's own testimony of Job to Satan was, "There is no one on earth like him; he is blameless and upright, a man who fears God and shuns evil." Job 2:3 As you read the life of Job, you will find that his godly life was lived out in meeting peoples' needs and he had powerful testimony of his Godly life. His walk with God was manifested in his walk with those around him. He was God's representative on this earth.

God's protection:

In Job 1:6 we read that the angels came to present themselves before the Lord. It says Satan came also. (Don't forget that Satan is a fallen angel, who is active and his demons are everywhere. Jesus called him the ruler of the air.) Satan said he had been roaming the earth. Satan was before God and this should not surprise us because in Revelation 12:10, says, "For the accuser (Satan) of our brothers, who accuses them before our God, day and night, has been hurled down."

Before we examine what was being said by Satan and God, it is important to hear what Satan says in Job 1:10. "Have you not put a hedge around him and his household and everything he has? You have blessed the work of his hands, so that his flocks and herds are spread throughout the land." Two things are very significant in what Satan testified to. First, God had put a hedge around Job and Satan could not get at him. Second, God had blessed him and Satan was not able to stop this blessing. Praise God! Satan finally spoke the truth and this reveals to us the power and blessing of a man being under God's life and reign.

Make no mistake about it; once man responds to God's salvation, he comes under God's reign and protection. In this world, with Satan's control and power, God's people can have a hedge around them to keep Satan out and live in God's blessing. From the time of Abraham all the way through Jesus and His body of believers, it has been God's will for His people to live under His protection. We see in the patriarchs, God's hand of protection blessing and leading them; God bringing His people out of Egypt and His protection was on them. Read Psalms 91. So many verses in that Psalm speak of God's protection. Twice in Jesus' prayer for all of His disciples, He prayed for their protection against the evil one. In John 17:15 Jesus said, "My prayer is not that you take them out of the world but protect them from the evil one." Job experienced God's complete protection and blessing on his life. This ought to be the normal way for God's people to live. Believers have been so used to Satan attacking them that they think it is something special to be under God's protection. God's protection has always been available to His people. It was never God's purpose for His people to live outside of His reign and protection so that Satan could attack them.

CHAPTER 5

Satan attacks Job

Satan came with the angels before God. He had been roaming the earth. Peter testified to Satan's activity in I Peter 5:8—"Your enemy the devil prowls around like a roaring lion looking for someone to devour." The Lord asked Satan, "Have you considered my servant Job?" This word "consider" in the Hebrew means to '**set upon**.' God was saying, Job 1:8 "Satan you have set yourself on My servant Job."

Then in Job 1:12, the Lord said to Satan, "Very well then, everything he has is in your hands, but on the man himself do not lay a finger." God was not giving Satan permission to attack Job but was stating a fact. Satan had found a way into Job's life and Job was then being attacked by Satan. Job still had God's protection concerning his physical body and life. God was not giving Satan permission to attack Job, but God was saying, Satan you have found a way into his life but on the man himself you cannot touch. There was nothing God could do to stop this attack. Satan had found a way into his life and he was going to do all the harm he could to this man of God.

Most believers have been taught that God was allowing Satan to attack Job. God was not allowing it but was acknowledging that Satan had set upon Job to find a way into his life. If God was allowing it, then He could have prevented it. This means the ultimate decision is in God's hands. If God could allow it or prevent it, then we have to conclude it was God's will for Job to receive these attacks. If we follow this line of thinking, then we must conclude that God had the ultimate decision to permit or prevent these attacks. This means it was God's will for Job to be attacked. Now, this is the very teaching that has left believers open to all kinds of attacks by the enemy. Satan loves to attack us and leave us believing that God has permitted it. Then we use Job as an example. Like Job, we end up with the outlook saying there is nothing we can do about it since it is from the Lord.

In the life of Jesus, we see an example of Satan's attack on Peter. The attack on Peter was somewhat the same as it was on Job. It was Jesus' last night with His disciples. Even on that final night they were arguing about who would be the greatest. Then Jesus said to Peter in Luke 22:31 "Simon, Simon, Satan has asked to sift you as wheat. But I have prayed for you Simon that your faith will not fail." Jesus was not giving Satan permission to attack Peter, but Jesus was saying to Peter, "Satan is set upon you to attack you, but I am praying for you." Satan found a way into

Peter's life and was able to attack Peter. Jesus said, "I am praying for you."

It is never God's will for Satan to attack his people; nor does He ever give Satan permission to do so. Jesus didn't say to Peter, "I give Satan permission to attack you." No! Jesus said the opposite, "I am praying for you." The only thing Jesus could do concerning Satan's attack on Peter was to pray for him. Jesus was not permitting this attack nor did His Father permit it. Peter, like Job, was in this world and Satan was looking for a way to attack him. The only thing Jesus could do was to pray for Peter. Jesus could not stop the attack, but He could take it to the heavenly realm and intercede on Peter's behalf. Jesus knew who was attacking Peter and He knew how to bring the life of the heavenly realm into the earth or natural realm by the prayer of faith.

Like Job, Jesus never gave a hint that Peter being attacked was allowed by His Father. Just as Jesus was not able to stop that attack on Peter. In the same way, God was not permitting Satan to attack Job, nor could God stop that attack. God never gives Satan permission to attack his people. Satan does not need God's permission as he seeks to devour, limit, and hinder our lives. In fact, if we really take the Word of God, we find that our Father has done everything to protect and keep us from the attacks of the evil one. He is not a God who allows evil to come into our lives, but a God who delivers us and protects us with His blessings. We are His special people and it has never been His will to give Satan permission to attack His people.

It has never been God's will to hurt or destroy His children. God ordained the family and what He ordains He will not give His permission for it to be destroyed. Then why would God give Satan permission to kill Job's children. He honors the family and it is not His will for it to be destroyed. God testified of Abraham, Genesis. 18:19 (NKJV) "For I have known him, in order that he may command his children and his household after him, that they keep the way of the Lord, to do righteousness and justice, that the Lord may bring to Abraham what He has spoken to him." Then in Malachi. 4:6 "And he shall turn the heart of the fathers to the children, and the heart of the children to their fathers, lest I come and smite the earth with a curse." God's will has always been to redeem man from the curse of sin not permit the curse. Galatians 3:13 "Christ hath redeemed us from the curse of the law, having become a curse for us: for it is written, cursed is every one who hangs on a tree."

Job's situation never changed until he stopped seeing God as the one who permitted it to happen and he began to take steps to correct it. It is the same for believers today. As long as we see God permitting these attacks of Satan and fail to go to God's Word on how to stop the attacks, then Satan's demons will be at us continually. Satan's goal in Job's life was his total destruction. That is, to curse God. And if Job had done that, then Satan would have taken his life.

After Job has lost everything and even all his children were taken from him, he spoke, "Naked I came from my mother's womb and naked I will depart. The Lord gave and the Lord has taken away, may the name of the Lord be praised." Job 1:21 It was not true that God had taken those things from him. It was purely the work of Satan. Then in Job 1:22 we read "in all of this, Job did not sin by charging God with wrongdoing." Job never charged God with doing wrong. however, Job saw it as from God. Even his wife and three friends, who came to help him, all thought that it was from God. Is this why many believers today look at Job and say God allowed it; which means He permitted it? Then, the only conclusion is it must be His will. God's whole work of redemption is to destroy Satan's work. Hebrews 2:14 says "so that by His death He might destroy him who holds the power of death—that is the devil." In I John 3:8, it says, "The reason the Son of God appeared was to destroy the devil's work." God said He came to destroy Satan's works, not to give him permission to work.

It is true that Job did not charge God with doing wrong, but he did praise God for something Satan had done. Job said, "the Lord has taken away, may the name of the Lord be praised." Never in Scripture are we to praise the Lord for Satan's work. We can praise God that He is able to work in the midst of Satan's attacks, but we do not praise God for what Satan does. Jesus never praised His Father for Satan's work. Read through Jesus' life and see the times that Jesus lifted His voice in praise. Never did He praise God commending Satan's work. It is not that believers today want to praise Satan; but like Job, we do not discern rightly between God's work and Satan's. It is then that we give God praise for what Satan has done. It is a sad commentary on our lives that people join in with Job in praising God for something that Satan has done. In John 10:10 Jesus said it is Satan who comes to kill, steal, and destroy. Jesus came to destroy Satan's work. Because these two facts are true, then God never gives Satan permission to attack His people. God's people have always been the apple of His eye, His treasured possession.

SATAN'S SECOND ATTACK ON JOB

Job's first reaction to these attacks was not in faith. Therefore, Satan was going to do all the damage to Job's life and testimony. Job praised the Lord for Satan's work, this is the opposite of faith In Job 2:3, it says Satan was again roaming the earth and he was able to "set upon" Job. God asked Satan the same question, "Have you considered (or "set upon") my servant Job?" Make no mistake about it, Satan was out to have Job curse God. In both attacks, Satan's stated purpose (Job 1:11 and 2:5) was to curse God. Satan's aim was to destroy God's testimony in the life of Job. This has always been Satan's work to steal, kill, and destroy. No wonder that Satan did not kill Job's wife because she was Satan's spokeswoman. In Job 2:9 she said, "curse God and die." Job had a powerful testimony in his walk with the Lord and Satan was out to destroy this testimony. Satan attacked Job's physical body but was not able to take his life.

Before the first attack, Job had God's complete

protection around his life and everything he had. Satan even admitted he was not able to get through. Once Satan found a way into Job's life, he then was able to set upon him and attack him. After the first attack, Job still had complete protection over his physical body and life. In the second encounter, Satan found a way to attack Job but was not able to take his life. This second attack of Satan left Job on the town trash heap with all sorts of sores and physical pain, not to mention all the emotional agony. His first words were that he cursed the day of his birth. In Job 3, the whole chapter, he questioned why he hadn't died at birth. This was not a testimony of a man who was trusting the Lord. Though he didn't curse God, Job did curse the day of his birth.

Job believed the attacks were from the Lord; therefore, he responded in cursing his life. He was saying, Lord, if this is your will for my life, then it would have been better if I had died at birth. What a pitiful sight! The man of God with such a powerful testimony had lost everything in his life, all his children were killed, he had physical pain from his bodily illness, emotionally drained and there he was sitting as an outcast on the town trash heap. Believers today say that God allowed or permitted that to happen to Job. But, if we are going to use Job as an example, let's ask these questions:

- How was Satan able to attack Job? Satan admitted that God had placed such a tight protection around him that he was not able to get at Job.

- What was Job able to do about those attacks and what are the things we can do about Satan's attacks on us?
- How did Job prevent those attacks from occurring again? And what can we do to prevent Satan's attack upon our lives?

CHAPTER 6

How Satan was Able
to Attack Job

In Job chapter 3, Job begins to speak to his three friends. In verse 25 Job said, "What I feared has come upon me, what I dreaded has happened to me." Fear in certain areas seems to be a controlling factor in Job's life.

Job was a man who believed God and his believing God built a strong protection around his whole life. Yet somehow, Satan got into Job's life. Was it through fear? There are two areas that speak of Job's fears. 'What I feared has come upon me'. He thought, ' what happens if I lose all my possessions?'. Another area of his fear is found in Job chapter 1, verses 4 and 5 that speaks of Job making sacrifices for his children. The revelation for sacrifices was given to Job by the Lord. Although he did the right thing, it was out of fear instead of faith. Job was responding to his children's actions out of fear instead of faith.

Now there are two results that fear produces in our lives. Firstly, is anxiety or worry. What you fear will be what you dwell on and this is worry. 'What if I get sick?' 'I will never have enough.' "What if my child gets on drugs.' Secondly, fear will have us speaking it to ourselves and to others. Without realizing it we are opening our lives to the ministry of the evil one. Our words are very powerful both for good and evil. Proverbs 18:21 (NKJV) "Death and life are in the power of the tongue and those who love it will eat it's fruit." One cannot think fear, speak fear and then expect good to come from it. The fruit of fear is it's fulfillment. So today, many believers know that fears are wrong, but we do not see how our fears are affecting and limiting our lives. At times, some believers seem to have the attitude, "Oh, well! We all have a little fear." This is kind of thinking and believing opens the way for Satan to gain a foothold in our lives. Do believers realize the harm and destructive work that fear produces in a life. Worry and anxiety are the results of fear. If we are fearing something then all we can do is be anxious or worry over it. Four times Scripture says, "the just will live by faith." This was Job's problem He had faith in God but he also had areas that he feared. "What happens if my children sin?" "What happens if I lose everything?" Instead of moving in faith he let fear control him in these areas.

My own testimony is that I have begun to see what the Scriptures say about fear. I never realized how Satan used fear in my life. Once I began to see what the Scriptures says about fear, and how Satan uses it. I became conscious of how in small areas of my life I was responding in fear. I never realized that in following the Lord fear was still operating in my life. It may have been small areas, but no matter how small, it was Satan's ministry. David said in Psalm 34:4"I sought the Lord and He answered me; and He delivered me from all my fears." One can never correct things in your life by fear. Many believers are like Job. They want to do the right thing, but they are being led by fear not by faith.

The only reason Job still had God's protection around his life to keep Satan from killing him was his faith. In all these attacks, Job testified Job 19:25 and 27 "I know my Redeemer lives...I myself will see Him." Job had faith and believed God for eternal life and he confessed it.

The area where Job still exercised faith, he had God's protection in keeping Satan from killing him. The areas in which Job had fear, he was attacked. Fear opens the door for attacks and faith builds a protection from the attacks. Eph.6:16 (NKJV) "Above all, taking the shield of faith, wherewith ye shall be able to quench all the fiery darts of the wicked." I John 5:4 "this is the victory that has overcome the world even our faith."

What does God say about Abraham in Genesis 18:19 "For I have chosen him, so that he will direct his children and his household after him to keep the way of the Lord by doing what is right and just." God testified of Abraham's faith in training his children. This verse showed Abraham was moving in faith by training his children; not like Job, who offered his sacrifices afraid they had sinned and he needed to make it right. Job's lack of trust opened the door to fear and his fear became greater than his faith in God.

There sat Job asking why is this happening to me. He even questioned why he did not die at birth. This man who had such a powerful testimony now sits, seeing himself defeated. He could not understand why these things were happening to him. In situations like this it is important that one comes into the light of God for it is only by the light that Satan is exposed and we can hear from God. This was just the opposite of Job's experience. Instead of his hearing from the Lord, read the first three chapters of Job and it is all about Job's eyes on himself. Then his three friends came to him and in their ministry they kept Job's eyes on himself. This only intensifies Job's desire to justify himself. Yet there were greater steps of God's relationship with Job that God wanted him to experience. If ever Job needed God's grace it was at this time. Job was asking the question why has this come upon me instead of asking the Lord to bring him into the light of His favor.

Faith is believing and acting upon God's Word. Either fear cancels out faith or faith overcomes fear. Man cannot live in faith and fear at the same time. Faith is the only way for man to respond to God. His faith was the only way he would receive God's grace. Rom. 4:16 (NKJV) "Therefore it is of faith that it might be according to grace." Without God's grace then there is no way man can relate to God. God spoke of Abraham's faith as he believed God's grace. It was totally God's favor that credited Abraham with righteousness. All Abraham had to do was believe for it is the only way to receive God's favor. When faith is removed then God's grace cannot be active in our lives. This is why Abraham is called the Father of all believers, he believed in God's grace to him and righteousness was credited to him. This is what God wanted to bring Job into even though he was a very good man and God spoke highly of Job. Yet there were areas that Job was trusting himself and his works and not the grace of God. This left him open to Satan's attacks. Fear was the result of his own works to please God. We referred to Peter being sifted by the devil. I had been teaching on God's grace and how Jesus still loved Peter even in his fall. I spoke of how he cursed and used foul language in denying Jesus. A few days later as I was walking my dog the Lord spoke to me, "Son, the sin was not just that Peter cursed in denying me but the root sin was that he didn't believe in my Grace toward him for he thought he had to do it in his own strength." Peter said to Jesus, "Even if all are made to stumble because of You, I will never be made to stumble." Peter was trusting what he must do to be accepted by Jesus. His own works left him open for Satan's attacks." Job moved in fear toward his children and his possessions. The root of Job's fear was not trusting God's grace to him. Just as Peter's cursing in denying Jesus was the result of his not trusting Jesus grace to him. Even Adam in eating of the tree was not believing God's favor to him.

All the good and godly acts of Job did not stop Satan tempting him with fear and then attacking him. God gave Job His revelation and all Job had to do was believe what

God revealed to him. Somehow Job believed his fears and they grew greater then his believing God's revelation. So today, many believers know that fears are wrong; but do not see the very root of fear is not trusting what Jesus has done for us. Fear is signal of our not believing what God can do. Satan is out to convince you not to believe God and so in the place of our faith in what God has done for us' Satan brings fear. It is said 'fear is placing our faith in the evil one." Fear is one of Satan's main tools to defeat and limit what God can do in a life.

What we can believe God for when facing fear.

The Word of God is clear God does not want His people to have any fear. 1John 4:18 (NKJV) "There is no fear in love; but perfect love casts out fear, because fear involves torment. But he who fears has not been made perfect in love." The word perfect in scripture means complete. In I John 4, eight times it mentions God's love to us. The law required us to love the Lord but grace gives us God's love. The beautiful thing about receiving God's perfect love is the more you receive the more you will love Him. Then in II Timothy 1:7 (NKJV) "For God has not given us the spirit of fear but of power and of love and of a sound mind." An unsound mind is controlled by fear. A sound mind is a mind controlled by the Spirit of God bringing His Word to us. If one has fear then bring it to the Lord knowing He loves you and delights to give you a sound mind. These two verses reveal that God by His love can give us victory over fear.

Understanding God's ministry to overcome fear.

Once I began to see what the Scriptures say about fear, and how Satan uses it; I became conscious of how in small areas of my life I was responding in fear instead of believing God's grace. I never realized that in following the Lord, that fear was still operating in my life. It may have been small areas; but no matter how small, I realized it was Satan's ministry. David said in Psalm 34:4 (NKJV) "I sought the Lord and He answered me; and He delivered me from all my fears." David overcame his fears not by trying to leave them but coming into God's love and favor.

We can never correct things in our lives by fear. Many believers are like Job. They may be doing the right thing, but they are being led by fear not by faith. Now, there are two very important points concerning Job's fear.

1. Job had God's revelation just as much as Noah or Abraham . God would not ask him to have faith in something that was not revealed to him.
2. God always reveals Himself and His ways to His people. The problem was not just the fear he had, but the lack of believing God's revelation to him.

If we go back to Satan's first attack, Job's response was, "the Lord gave and the Lord has taken away, may the

Name of the Lord be praised." First, it was not true that God had taken those things from Job. However, Job saw it that way and said, "It is of the Lord. There is not much I can do about it – I'll just praise the Lord." This was Job's reaction. Yet after Satan's second attack Job curses the day of his birth. Job 3:1 "After this Job opened his mouth and cursed the day of his birth." This is not faith responding but self-pity. In fact, it seems after these attacks Job had less faith. Job was responding in a negative way and Satan was making sure those fears came to fulfillment.

Do you see Job, the man who had such a powerful testimony, now having lost all things, children, health, and cast out sitting on the town dump. In that state, he had even lost all hope as he cursed the day of his birth. This is fear's fruit and his confession of hopelessness.

Hope comes to us from God's revelation and then we exercise faith to believe the word of hope to be fulfilled. If God allows us to be destroyed, then how can we have hope in Him? That was Job's dilemma. How could he exercise faith when he saw God as the source of these attacks? No wonder he cursed the day of his birth. If God permitted those attacks, then there was no word of hope and no faith to believe God to fulfill that hope.

The life of Job is not exhorting us to understand defeat and disaster in our lives as the will of our Father, but as the work of the enemy. When believers see these as God allowing them, which means He is permitting them, then they run to and hide behind Romans 8:28 "And we know that in all things God works for the good of those who love

Him, who have been called according to His purpose." It does not matter what the enemy has hit them with, they often stand on this verse.

Yet in this verse it mentions God's purpose. First, it has never been God's purpose to destroy families. This is the enemy's work. All of Scripture teaches us that God's people are set apart as special. They are under God's blessings. Job had a very powerful testimony with all those who lived around him and Satan was out to destroy that testimony.

Often believers use Romans 8:28 concerning all things working for the good. There are two responses that we must avoid. One being that God is behind the attacks. God never attacks His people for the scripture is clear that every good gift comes from our Father and it is Satan who attacks to steal, kill and destroy. These attacks are not from the Lord. Yet God assures us that in these attacks He is for us and can work on our behalf. He can turn what Satan has brought on us into His fullness and reign. Secondly, believers respond to these attacks as if God is attacking us to teach us. For any attack, a serious illness or accident, believers often say, "Oh, God is teaching me." There is one and only one way God has ever taught His people and that is through His Word. No illness, no accident, no curse of sin will teach us of the Lord. His ways can only come to us by His Word. Now, what happens if we have an illness and are confined to bed? Then we have time to hear from the Lord. God can turn that illness that is Satan's curse and bring forth his blessing. It is not the illness that teaches us but the Word of God. This is why it is so vital that we hear the Word that builds our faith before the enemy attacks.

I heard a well known Christian leader mention about one who went through some serious illness and how close it drew him to the Lord. Then he said, "I will never be that close to the Lord for I have not experienced anything like that." What he was saying, 'my experience draws me closer to the Lord.' Only God's grace given to us in Jesus draws us close to the Lord. I have the opportunity to walk in His love and fullness today. I don't need a negative experience to draw me closer. I have a jail ministry and I have had men say to me, "The Lord has brought me in here and now I am walking with the Lord." Praise God that their eyes are now turned onto the Lord and they are responding to Him! I tell them wrong decisions has brought them to this place not God. God can take this time in jail to minister to you through His Word. It is good that they are hearing from God. God is able to minister through anything that happens to us. The good news is we can respond to God before Satan attacks us. We don't have to experience any of these things to be drawn to God. His Word, His life, and all that He has for us is the same for us even before we receive the attacks of Satan. What God can do in our lives after these attacks, He can do for us before they ever happen. It is not the attacks that draw us closer to the Lord, but hearing His Word. Often because of attacks, our ears are turned onto the Lord to hear from Him. But God forbid that we need attacks to turn our eyes on the Lord or to grow!

Believers use the argument that God is teaching them and then they back it up with Job's life. They have not meditated on Job's whole life. If they do, they will see that Job was not helped until His eyes were turned onto the Lord and he heard the words of God. We will see it was not Job's experience that helped him, but the word of the Lord.

Believers must realize that God's purpose for their lives is to represent Christ and His reign. Romans 5:17 This verse states God's purpose for His people—"For if, by the trespass of the one man, death reigned through that one man, how much more will those who receive God's abundant provision of grace and of the gift of righteousness reign in life through the one man, Jesus Christ." God's purpose has always been for His people to reign on this earth as His representatives. Job reigned on this earth as God's representative, but Satan was out to destroy that reign. Is this God's reign in Job's life to be sitting outside the city on a pile of garbage, cursing the day of his birth? God reigned in Job's life before these attacks and again after the attacks; but during the attacks, Satan was reigning. It is never God's will or purpose, nor does God allow or permit Satan to attack and reign in a believer's life.

My wife and I know what it is to be attacked by Satan in our family. A number of years ago a member of our family was in a very serious car accident. Looking at the picture of the car, you would wonder how anyone could have come out of it alive. At the same time, two of our children went through some very personal attacks in their marriages. Both of these were not the normal problems that married couples face. Plus, there was another personal area that caused us a lot of heartbreaking problems. We were believers. We were walking with the Lord. Yet, I realized from the Word of God that these attacks were not from the Lord and He was not trying to teach me something through them.

I began to seek the Lord and learn all I could about faith, hearing from God, and how I could receive His protection that He has promised in His Word. I didn't want to hear or preach a nice sermon. I needed to hear the Word of the Lord. I needed to grow in my believing God's Word and what He says about His people. I didn't want to hear another leader water down the Word of God and give me excuses of why God allows these things. I needed faith and I was hungry for it. I wanted to hear men whose teachings believed that what God says is possible.

As I meditated on the Word of God, I approached it believing that God can do what He says. I didn't approach it from the common viewpoint that we can't understand why these things happen or we can't really understand the Lord's ways. That is Satan speaking and if you look at the life of Jesus; His main ministry was to reveal His Father, His Father's love, purpose, and His Kingdom reign on this earth. From creation until now, it has never been God's purpose to hide His life and purposes from man but to give man a full revelation of Himself.

Like Job, these attacks on our family were not because we had great sins; just the opposite. We loved the Lord. We wanted to serve Him the best we could. We were faithful in the things of the Lord. Yet Satan attacked us as he did Job. One thing I realized was that these attacks were not from God nor did He allow them. I realized God was for us and His favor was upon us and I knew God could take these attacks by Satan to bring forth His grace. I know that God is able to have His people abound in every situation. All answers and understanding do not come instantly but they come as our focus stands firmly on walking by faith, believing God's Word and having the Lord's protection around us.

Whatever attack you or your family have experienced, do not in any way credit God with it. God is not the cause but the answer to Job's attacks. The reason why so many believers never move in victory is because they see God as the cause of the attack, not the answer to it. However, He never approaches us in condemnation because Satan has attacked us. It is bad enough for us to be attacked by the enemy; so God does not come along and pour on us the weight of condemnation. The glorious truth is that is why Jesus came. That is why we have His Word, so that we won't be condemned; but be delivered to live in His victory over the enemy.

God was not condemning Job for his fear. But He did want Job to have victory over those fears. God knew all the good things He had for Job. And if Job was moving in fear instead of faith, then he was limiting what God could do in His life. As we will see, Job lost all hope that God was for him. He felt condemned. Plus his three friends just poured condemnation on him. Satan will use our thoughts, our words and even people to pour on condemnation. This is why God sent His Son into the world, to deliver us from Satan's grip and to live the abundant life. John 3:17

Whatever has taken place in your life, you need to realize God's love is for you. God's love for you will never promote Satan's attacks. Nor will His love condemn you if Satan does attack you. God is the promoter of life and blessings. Satan is against you. He will do everything he can to destroy your testimony. Job went real low, but once he realized God was for Him, things began to change.

Once we see that God is for us, no matter how hard Satan hits us; then we will respond to God, not as the promoter of evil, but as the only One who can defeat the evil attacks. Satan is very subtle and he knows how to attack God's people. This is why we need to hear the Word of God. Some of Satan's attacks will not be exposed unless the light is turned on. The revelation of the Word of God needs to be turned on in these areas. Once the light was turned on in Job's life, he again experienced God's blessings. If Satan has attacked us, then it does not disqualify us from God's blessings. Job experienced God's restoration in a very powerful way and so can you.

THREE THINGS GOD REVEALS TO US CONCERNING SATAN'S ATTACKS

We need to be sensitive to the Holy Spirit and the Word of God concerning Satan's attacks. Protection is possible, but believers must learn to walk in that protection. There are three main things concerning Job's protection from God. As we understand these things, we will be able to appropriate God's protection for our lives.

1. The attacks of Satan are not from God or permitted by Him. Job needed to see that God was not against him, but for him. It was hard for Job to see God as the One who allowed these things and then have a solid faith to overcome them. Once we see these attacks are from Satan, then we can respond to God's Word and gain the victory. It is important to see what the Scriptures say about Satan. In each passage, you do not read of God giving Satan permission; but, just the opposite, of how Jesus defeated Satan. Satan is defeated and we can walk in God's blessings.

> Ephesians 6:16—"In addition to all this, take up the shield of faith, with which you can extinguish all the flaming arrows of the evil one." (This verse points to how we can stop Satan.)

> I Peter 5:8–9—"Your enemy the devil prowls around like a roaring lion looking for someone to devour. Resist him." (Satan is after us and we are to resist him.)

The following three verses speak of Jesus destroying Satan's power and work; not promoting it.

Hebrews 2:14—"By His death He might destroy him who holds the power of death that is the devil."

Colossians 2:15—"And having disarmed the powers and authorities, He made a public spectacle of them triumphing over them by the cross."

I John 3:8—"The reason the Son of God appeared was to destroy the devils works."

All these verses speak directly of the evil one; and never do we read of God permitting Satan to act. In fact, all of these verses speak just the opposite; of how God wants to expose, defeat and give us victory over the enemy. James tells us that God cannot be tempted with evil. Then why would we associate God with permitting evil? Evil has never been God's purpose for man nor does God give Satan permission to attack a believer.

2. Believers are promised God's protection. Job knew what it was to have God's protection. His faith provided the seal around him and Satan was not able to penetrate it. The key for our protection is not how much faith a believer has but are they exercising faith. Faith must always be active in a believer's life; and as faith is active, it will grow.

Abraham lived about the same time as Job lived. God related to Abraham by faith. And this is how God relates to everyone. In fact, Abraham is called the father of faith.

The Word says Abraham is the father of all believers. Abraham's first step of faith was to leave his country and relatives and go to the land God would show him. Toward the end of Abraham's life, God tells him to sacrifice his son Isaac. Of course this later step of faith was greater than just leaving his country. God honored Abraham's first step of faith as much as the later one. God honored his faith at the beginning of his life as much as his faith in being willing to sacrifice his Son. Be assured it is not how much faith you have or how mature it is but that you begin to believe God's revelation to you. In God's sight, Abraham's faith at the beginning of his life was just as mature as it was at the end of his life.

Once we realize the value of walking in faith, then our first steps of faith will give us the same protection as greater steps of faith. Abraham had God's protection, not because of his mature faith, but because his faith was active. It was the same for Job. He had God's protection because of his faith. Satan was able to break through that protection; not because God willed or permitted it, but that Satan found a way into Job's life. It was not a question of how mature Job's faith was but that his faith was mixed with fear.

3. Learn to walk in faith before Satan's attacks. Job did not respond in faith after these attacks. Don't wait for a crisis that is Satan's attack for you to obtain faith. God wants His people learning to believe and move on His

Word before the attacks. Then, when the attacks take place, we will know how to use our faith.

I have already mentioned how Satan really hit my life and family. I was learning to grow in faith when these attacks hit me. I had much to learn. But once I identified them as Satan's attacks, I knew the direction I needed to move in faith. I knew God's Word was true and I could trust what He would speak to me. I don't want to wait for the attacks of the enemy to learn how to walk in faith. I am learning before his attacks. Yes, Job did regain his faith and once again he had God's protection and blessing. But who wants to experience what Job experienced? Why should we have to experience an attack from the devil to grow in faith? Romans 10:17 (NJKV) "Faith comes by hearing and hearing by the Word of God."

CHAPTER 7

Job's Response to the Counsel of his three Friends.

First, it is at this point in our study of Job that we need to look at his life before these attacks and see what it was like. Second, we need to look at what his life was like during these attacks. It was during these attacks that three of Job's friends came to help him; however, instead of helping him, they just poured condemnation on him.

WHAT WAS JOB'S LIFE LIKE BEFORE THESE ATTACKS

It was hard for Job to understand why those things were happening to him because he really had a heart to live for the Lord. Scripture speaks of Job, saying that his life was upright, righteous, and blameless. This means he always wanted to do the right thing. Scripture says Job trusted God and shunned evil. We read that God said the same thing twice about Job. (Job 1:8 and Job 2:3).

In both of those verses, the Lord said "There is no one on earth like Job." When God testified of Job in this way we know his life was a powerful testimony. God mentioned that Job shunned evil. Look in Job 31:1. Job testified of his shunning evil. "I made a covenant with my eyes, not to look lustfully at a girl." This man knew God's hand was upon his life in such a powerful way that he made a covenant not to lust after women. Job 29:14 speaks of him putting on righteousness and justice as his clothing.

Now, if Job was a righteous man, it would have been seen in his walk and life on this earth. His faith in God would have led him to live God's life on this earth before his fellow countrymen. The following paragraph is taken from Job 29. First, Job testified to his intimate friendship with God that blessed his house. It was a known fact that when Job went to the gate of the city that the young men stepped aside and the older men stood up.

> "The chief men refrained from speaking. Those who heard me spoke well of me. I rescued the poor who cried for help and the fatherless who had no one to help him. I was eyes to the blind and feet for the lame. I was a father to the needy. I took up the case of the stranger. I was against the wicked and helped those who came under

their power. Men waited for me to speak and after I spoke, they had nothing else to say. Men were glad to consider me chief and king among the troops. I was one who comforted the mourners." (excerpts from Job's testimony- Job 29: 7-17)

In chapters 29 and 31, Job mentioned how he lived his life and what he had done for others. He was not bragging, for those men knew what his life was like. He was known in the entire East and people could not deny that Job was a good and godly man. His godly life was seen in how he treated others. He knew he had a heart for God and wanted to honor God in all things, so it was very difficult for him to understand why he experienced these attacks. Job was not bragging, but was saying, I have always wanted to live a righteous life. His testimony was not just before the Lord, but was very powerful before his fellow men.

JOB'S LIFE DURING THE ATTACKS

What was Job's life like after the attacks? We know that all of his children had been killed. He had lost all of his possessions. His body was full of sores and he ended up sitting on the town's trash heap. There was not only the physical suffering, but also emotional suffering and turmoil. In Job 30:9–12, we read that Job, the man who wanted to always help those in need, was receiving mocking; and some were spitting in his face. Many wanted to see Job destroyed. They seemed to gloat in his suffering.

This was now Job's testimony. Job 19:17–20 "My breath is offensive to my wife; I am loathsome to my own brothers. Even the little boys scorn me, when I appear they ridicule me. All my intimate friends detest me and those I love have turned against me. I am nothing but skin and bones." Job 30:16–17 "And now my life ebbs away; days of suffering grip me. Night pierces my bones, my gnawing pains never rest."

My! Satan had done everything he could to destroy Job and his powerful testimony. In spite of all that Satan hit him with, let's not forget that Job had been in a place of victory. But, before he came to a place of restoration, he was hit with more suffering in the form of condemnation. Satan has not only knocked Job down but keeps pounding him with condemnation. Not only does Satan attack believers, but then he pours condemnation and guilt on them. In that horrible situation, Job was then condemned by those who came to help him. This man needed hope; not condemnation. Is it any wonder that Job responded the way he did by trying to justify himself?

JOB'S ENCOUNTER WITH HIS THREE FRIENDS

Job's three friends heard about his situation and went to see him. Job chapters 3 through 31 are a discourse between Job and his three friends. Each of these men spoke to Job and Job then spoke to them. Eliphaz and Bildad spoke three times to Job and Zophar spoke twice.

We will look at what each of those men said to Job and then see Job's response to them.

Job spoke first. In chapter 3, Job began by cursing the day of his birth. Over and over, he kept saying, "Why was I born?" Job 3:11 (NKJV) "It would have been better if I were stillborn." Job was a man who trusted God and yet he failed to respond in faith. How can Job curse the day of his birth and at the same time have faith in God's hand upon his life?

It was after Job made those statements that his three friends began to speak to him. His three friends had heard about Job's life and had come to comfort him. When they saw Job, they could hardly recognize him. Scripture says they wept, tore their cloths, and poured dust on their heads. They sat for seven days and nights before they even spoke a word.

These three men had one main theme. Job you have sinned and these things that have happened to you are the result of your evil ways. Over and over, these men poured condemnation on Job and said that God was against him, which led Job to try and justify himself. The more condemnation they poured on Job, the more he tried to justify himself and wanted to appear before God to prove his godly life.

Eliphaz was the first to speak. He spoke three times. He spoke in chapter 4, 15, and 22. What was amazing was that he began by commending Job in Job 4:3–4. This one incident is the only time that any of them spoke positively about Job. Yet in the same speech he also condemned Job.

Elephaz:

> Job 4:7—He said no innocent person ever perished or the upright destroyed.

> Job 4:8—You have plowed evil and now are reaping it.

> Job 4:17—Man cannot be righteous in God's sight!

> Job 5:1–3—Call and see if anyone or even an angel will hear you.

> Job 5:3–4—He referred to Job as being a fool. (Remember a fool is one who forgets God.)

> Job 5:12–13—He accused Job of acting with craftiness to God so God could not bless him.

> Job 5:17—God is disciplining you so do not despise the discipline of God.

In Eliphaz's counsel to Job, he accused Job of sin. And because of sin, God was not hearing Job but disciplining him. Now that only dug deeper into Job's thoughts that God was against him. When he says to Job in Job 4:17 "can a mortal be more righteous then God". What he failed to say is God can impart righteousness to man. God did this for Abraham. Gen. 15:6 Job needed to know God was for him not against him. If God was against him, that killed any hope that he could exercise faith in God.

Job's response:

> Job 6:1–2—Job responded that if all of his calamities and anguish could be weighed, it would outweigh the sand of the sea.

> Job 6:9—It would be better if God would kill me.

> Job 6:10—I would have this joy had I not denied the words of the Holy One.

> Job 6:24—Teach me and tell me my faults and I will be quiet and listen to you.

> Job 7:7—Job confessed he would never see happiness again.

> Job 7:20—I despise my life.

> Job 7:20—If I have sinned, then what wrong have I done to you.

Note how Job's words revealed that his eyes were on himself. No one will ever be helped whose eyes are on themselves for this only leads to self-pity. Job's solution would never be found while his focus was on the problem. Plus you will note the counsel of his three friends kept his eyes on himself. This only increased his self-pity.

It was answers to his problems that he needed, not the magnifying his problems.

Bildad:

> Job 8:2–3—Your words are only wind. No substance or truth is in them. God does not pervert justice nor does He pervert what is right.

> Job 8:6—If you were pure and right, God would restore you to your rightful place.

> Job 8:13—You have forgotten God and you are just like the godless.

> Job 8:20—God will not reject a blameless man.

Job was down and these men were pouncing on him. Bildad told Job that he was not a blameless man, for if he was, then God would restore him. What he was saying to Job was to clean his life and God would accept him. No one can cleanse his life and then come to God. God always relates to man by His grace and it is by His grace that He cleanses us. We don't get clean to come to Him. We come to Him to be cleansed. Bildad failed to know God's grace.

Job's response:

> Job 9:2–3—Can a man be righteous before God? Can man dispute or argue with God?

Job then spoke of God being the all powerful and the knowing One.

> Job 9:15—"Though I were innocent, I could not answer him".

> Job 9:16—Even if I summoned God and He responded, I don't think He would listen to me.

> Job 9:24—God gave the world to the wicked; and if God didn't do it, who did?

> Job 9:32—He is not like man that I may go to court and debate with Him.

> Job 9:33—There is no one who can go between us. arbitrate between us and represent us both.

> Job 10:2—I would say to God, "Do not condemn me, but tell me what charges you have against me."

> Job 10:8—You formed and made me. Will those same hands now destroy me?

Job had lost all hope. He believed God was against him. God would not give him a hearing and there was no one who could go between the two. Job was crying out for a mediator. Is there someone who can go to God on my behalf?

Zophar:

> Job 11:4–5—You say you are pure in your sight. How I wish that God would speak that He would open His lips against you.

> Job 11:6— "God has even forgotten some of your sins".

> Job 11:14— "If you put away the sin that is in your hand and allow no evil to dwell in your tent".

> Job 11:15—"Then you will lift up your face without shame".

All three of those men were charging Job with sin and claiming that they were backed by God. This counsel kept Job's eyes on himself. Their counsel to Job was on sin and nothing about about what he could believe God to do for him..

Job's response:

> Job 12:3—Twice Job said that he was not inferior to them. (Job 13:2)

> In chapter 12 Job spoke of the greatness of God.

> Job 13:3— "I desire to speak to the Almighty and to argue my case with God".

> Job 13:15— "Though He slay me, yet will I hope in Him; I will surely defend my ways to His face".

> Job 13:23–24— "How many wrongs and sins have I committed? Show me my offense and my sin. Why do you hide your face and consider me your enemy?"

What was so tragic about Job's friends was that their counsel to Job was telling him that God was against him. They wanted to prove Job was wrong more than they wanted to help him. That was why over and over Job stated He wanted to go into God's presence and plead his case because he was told God was doing that to him. Neither Job nor these three men saw the evil one behind these attacks. This is why Job needed to hear what he could believe God to do for him.. Only his believing will bring him out of all these attacks.

Eliphaz:

> Job 15:3— "Would he argue with useless words and speeches that have no value?"

> Job 15:5–6— "Your sin prompts your mouth. Your own mouth condemns you not mine".

> Job 15:9— "What do you know that we do not know? What insights do you have that we do not have?"

Job 15:10— "The gray-haired and the aged are on our side, men even older than you father".

Job 15:14— "What is man that he could be pure, or one born of woman that he could be righteous?"

Job 15:15–16— "If God places no trust in His holy ones, if even the heavens are not pure in His eyes, how much less man, who is vile and corrupt,"

Job 15:25— "because he shakes his fist at God and vaunts himself against the Almighty,"

There seems to have been a lot of jealousy with these men toward Job. In Job 15:10 They claimed they had wisdom because they were backed with men who were old and their age gave them wisdom. They even accused Job of shaking his fist at God.

Job's response:

Job 16:2—…"miserable comforters are you all."

Job 16:4–5 "I also could speak like you, if you were in my place; I could make fine speeches against you and shake my head at you. But my mouth would encourage you; comfort from my lips would bring you relief".

Job 16:11–15— "God has turned me over to evil men; and thrown me into the clutches of the wicked". (Job was thinking that God had handed him over to Satan and he could not understand God's motive in doing that.)

Job 16:19–21— Is there someone in heaven that will stand up for me and take my side? I want someone to plead to God for me as a man pleads for his friend. THIS IS AN IMPORTANT PASSAGE. We will refer to it later.

Job 17:2—I watch as everyone mocks me.

This was the second time that Job spoke of a mediator between himself and God. Down deep inside, Job thought he wanted to bring his case before God and argue it. He had no hope that there was a mediator between him and God. We will see that there came a time that he was given the revelation of a mediator.

Bildad:

Job 18:2— "When will you end these speeches? Be sensible and then we can talk".

> Job 18:5— The lamp of the wicked is
> snuffed out. The flame of his fires stops
> burning"

He then speaks of all the things that happen to the wicked.

> Job 18:17— "The memory of him perishes
> and he has no name in the land".

> Job 18:21— :Surely such is the dwelling of
> an evil man and such is the place of one
> who knows not God".

It was the same old theme: that Job was nothing but a wicked man and he was experiencing the fruit of his sins. That was all they could say to Job. They never spoke of restoration and how it could be obtained. All they could do was point their finger at Job as a sinner. No message of grace, faith or hearing from God – watch when sin is the main theme of a ministry.

Job's response:

> Job 19:6-7—God has wronged me, though
> I cry I've been wronged; I get no response.
> When I call for help there is no justice.

> Job 19:11—His anger burns against me.
> He counts me among His enemies.

Job 19:25–27— "I know that my Redeemer lives and that in the end He will stand upon the earth. Yet in my flesh I will see God. I myself will see Him with my own eyes".

Job's response was that God was doing that to him. He felt he was being treated wrongly by God and that he didn't deserve it. Yet he still had faith in God as his redeemer. His faith in God broke through all his sufferings and the condemnation of those three men.

Zophar:

Job 20:5— "The mirth of the wicked is brief, the joy of the godless lasts but a moment".

Job 20:12— "Though evil is sweet in his mouth and he hides it under his tongue".

Job 20:19— "For he oppressed the poor and left them destitute; he had seized houses he did not build".

Job 20:23—To the sinful man, "God will vent His burning anger against him and rain down blows upon him".

Job 20:29— "Such is the fate God allots the wicked".

This is one of the few places (Job 20:19) that he accused

Job of certain sins. If you read Job chapters 29 and 31, you find the very opposite of Job's life. Of all the people, he was the one who was always helping those in need.

Job's response:

Job 21:7–21 tells us to look at the wicked. Often they are not experiencing these things. They seem to prosper and yet they have no desire for God. Job tried to tear down their arguments and submit that it was not sin that had caused all these things to happen.

Eliphaz:

Job 22:3— "What pleasure would it give the Almighty if you were righteous? What would He gain if your ways were blameless?"

Job 22:5— "Is not your wickedness great and your sins endless?"

Job 22:6— "You demanded security from your brothers for no reason; you stripped men of their clothing leaving them naked."

Job 22:12— "Is not God in the heights of heaven?"

Job 22:14— "Thick clouds veil him, so he does not see us as He goes about in the vaulted heavens."

Job 22:23— "If you return to the Almighty, you will be restored; if you remove wickedness far from your tent."

Job 22:30— "He will deliver even one who is not innocent, who will be delivered through the cleanness of your hands?"

This was Eliphaz's last speech to Job. He states that God has no pleasure in one's being righteous (Job 22:3). What was God's testimony of Abraham? God credited to Abraham righteousness. It says he was a friend of God. He is the Father of all who believe. Abraham, who lived during this time and God's work of righteousness was effective in his life. In Ephesians 1, Scripture tells us it is God's pleasure to see man made righteous.

Job's response:

Job 23:3–4"If only I knew where to find him. If only I could go to His dwelling. I would state my cause before Him and fill my mouth with arguments."

Job 23:10–12— "He knows the way I take. When He has tested me, I will come forth as gold. My feet have closely followed His steps. I have kept to His way without turning aside. I have not departed from the commands of His lips. I have treasured the word of His mouth more than my daily bread."

Job 23:16— "God has made my heart faint; the Almighty has terrified me.'

Job 24—In this chapter Job tells all the things a wicked man will do. Job 24:25 "If this is not so, who can prove me false and reduce my words to nothing?"

Job believed God knew all about him. Job 23:10-12 – Job's faith seems to come to the surface when he believed God would bring him forth as gold.

Bildad

Job 25:4–5— "How can a man be righteous before God? How can one born of woman be pure? If even the moon is not bright and the stars are not pure in His sight?"

Job 25:6— 'How much less man, who is but a maggot, a son of man who is only a worm?"

Is he saying it is impossible for man to ever be righteous in God's sight? Was he saying God who created man in His image is only a maggot? Sin has destroyed man's image but this is what God's salvation is all about to bring man back into His image. Not to magnify man as a maggot.

Job's final response to these three men.

Job 26:2–4— "How you have helped the powerless? How you have saved the arm that is feeble? What advice have you offered to one without wisdom/ And what great insight have you displayed? Who has helped you utter these words? And whose spirit spoke from your mouth?"

Job 27:2— 'As surely as God lives, who had denied me justice, the Almighty who has made me tastes bitterness of soul.'

Job 27:3–4— 'As long as I have life within me, the breath of God in my nostrils my lips will not speak wickedness and my tongue will utter no deceit."

Job 27:5–6— "I will not deny my integrity; I will maintain my righteousness and never let go of it; my conscience will not reproach me as long as I live."

Job 29:4–5— "I was in my prime when God's intimate friendship blessed my house when the Almighty was still with me."

Job 31:1— "I made a covenant with my eyes not to look lustfully at a girl."

Job 31:6— "Let God weigh me in honest scales and he will know that I am blameless."

Job was experiencing total rejection. Everyone had turned against Job; his wife, his friends, and even the young boys were rejecting Job. These men brought more condemnation on Job by telling him that God only did these things to him because of his sin. Job could not understand it because in his heart, he had surrendered to the Lord. Yet he could not understand the attacks nor the condemnation of these men.

CHAPTER 8

Three Friends view of God determines their Counsel to Job

These men were not able to help Job because their revelation of God was totally wrong. If one's revelation of God is wrong, then they will not be able to know God's work and ministry in their lives. It was God who said their counsel was wrong! **Twice** in Job 42:7–8 God said their view of God was wrong, "You have not spoken of me what is right." Job was asked to pray for them, God said of these three men, "I will not deal with you according to your folly."

Amplified Bible—"for you have not spoken of Me the thing that is right."

Living Bible—"you have not been right in what you have said about me."

King James—"you have not spoken of Me the thing that is right."

If they failed to understand the character of God, then

how could they understand the ways of God? When one fails to understand God then they will never know God's ways. Their counsel to Job was totally wrong because their knowledge of God was wrong.

First step of their wrong view of God: God is against you!

Their counsel to Job was that God was doing it to him for his sin; therefore, God was against him. Was God really against Job after all the good things He said about him. We know that those attacks were by Satan and Satan alone. God does not allow Satan to attack his people. Satan will always look for a way to attack believers. Jesus spoke in Matthew 12:22–32 that no kingdom divided against itself can stand. In this passage, the Pharisees said that Jesus had done those miracles by the power of the devil. Jesus made it clear that no kingdom can be divided. He was speaking of His kingdom and Satan's kingdom. They cannot be mixed.

God does not do the work of the devil nor does the devil do the work of God. Satan wants us to believe that his works are of God. This is why God has given to His people the spirit of discernment, which is to distinguish what is of God and what is of Satan. These men were attributing Satan's attacks to God. And because they said God was doing that to Job, what hope did Job have that God could work in his life. If God was doing that to Job (or even permitting it to happen), then what hope did Job have that God would remove it? This kills hope and faith in God. If He is a God who permits this, then how can I trust Him to deliver me? If God permits Satan's attacks, then God is against me. Once a person feels God is against them, then there is no hope and no faith for God to work in their lives.

See Deuteronomy 1. The children of Israel didn't go into the promise land because they believed God hated them. That would mean God was against them and was not for them. Once they believed that God was against them, they had no faith to enter the land God promised them. If we see that those attacks were by Satan (not God), then there is hope that God can do something about it. Satan is against me. He is the thief, the destroyer, and the killer; but God is for me. He is my deliverer. This is why Job was stuck in such a rut of trying to justify himself. Job was being told over and over that God was against him. Job had faith enough to testify, "I know my redeemer lives.", but his faith was never helped or activated by telling him God was against him. Job's faith never rose during the speeches of his three friends.

No person will rise up in faith who feels that God is against them. No matter what attacks Job had or that we may experience, never loose sight of the fact that God is for you. Once anyone feels God is against them, all hope is gone. The very thing Job needed to hear was God is for him and He knew what was taking place in his life. He is concerned and can come to your aid. Hearing God's revelation that He loves man and His will is to redeem men; this builds faith.

Second step of their wrong view of God: They were more sin conscious than righteous conscious.

In the book of Job, 27 chapters are about Job's three friends and his answer to them. Their basic counsel to Job was, 'these things are happening to you because of your sins'. This kept Job in a feeling of condemnation to the point he wanted to justify himself. Many of the things of which Job was accused was just the opposite of his actions. A sin focused counsel never brings one into the light of God's revelation. Now if there is any sin then it can only be exposed by the light of God's revelation.Remember Job lived about the same time as Abraham. Abraham received God's revelation of grace so he could fulfill God's purpose for His life.

Yet these men made sin the big issue between Job and God. Today believers make sin the big issue between them and God. In redemption sin is what God takes from us and it says, "He remembers them no more." Righteousness is what God gives to us. Yet most believers think and focus on what God has taken from them then the Righteousness He gives to them. I know what it is like to have more faith in my sinning instead of believing that I am the righteous in Christ. Without realizing it the more we focus on our sin and see our selves sinning the more we will sin. Our focus and emphasizes on sin will not give us victory over it. This is what brings condemnation and frustration to so many believers. In Job 32:3 the fourth man Elihu said, "they had found no answer yet condemned Job." A sin focused life will always keep one under condemnation.

I talk to many believers and they have heard messages and teaching on sin but they have very little revelation of being righteous. If a believer is not living out of His righteousness then he will always struggle with sin. You do not defeat sin by focusing on it but by the righteousness that God has imparted to you. If the body of Christ today heard as much teaching on Christ making us righteous as they do on sin then we would see the victory that God has provided for us. Romans.5:17

Job needed to hear the Word of the Lord that righteousness was credited to him by his believing. Anyone who comes into the Light of God's revelation will have their sins exposed. A good example is in Isaiah 6. Isaiah admitted his sin, but that was after he had seen the Lord. The light was turned on and his sins were then exposed. None of those three men turned God's light of revelation on Job, yet they condemned him. The more you focus on sin, the more your eyes are on yourself. This was Job's experience with the counsel of these three men. He was told over and over of his sin and was never told of his righteousness. So his eyes were on himself trying to prove he had not sinned.

Under the New Covenant of grace, we are made righteous. It is no longer credited to us but we are made righteous by Christ. We have His righteousness. God has not only taken care of the sin issue but in so doing removes all condemnation. These men kept Job under condemnation and much of teaching today on sin keeps believers under condemnation. In God's Word, Romans.

8:1 says "Therefore, there is now no condemnation to those who are in Christ Jesus." In John 8:11 we hear of the lady taken in adultery. When all her accusers had left, Jesus said to her, "Neither do I condemn you go and sin no more." (NKJV) He first removed all condemnation and then He said you can have victory over sin. The emphases today is overcome sin and you won't be condemned but God removes condemnation so we can have victory.

The great issue with God is not sin, but man's reconciliation with Him. If God was going to reconcile man to Himself then the sin issue had to be removed. It is no longer a barrier between God and man. His total forgiveness opens the way for man to be reconciled to God. Sin is an issue to man and barrier between him and God. This barrier is removed when man believes in God's forgiveness for his sins. On God's part forgiveness has already been accomplished; on man's part it is his acceptance of Christ's forgiveness that completes the reconciliation.

When we say sin is not an issue to God, we are not making light of sin but magnifying the glorious death and resurrection of our Lord Jesus Christ. All judgment for sin was placed on Jesus once and for all. II Corinthians. 5:19 says, "God was reconciling the world to Himself in Christ, not counting men's sins against them." The very sacrifice of Jesus took all of the punishment for sin. His death was not only the physical suffering but the emotional weight of all sins being placed on Him. In the garden He sweated great drops of blood. Sin was a very big issue to God and by His love and favor He has provided forgiveness. This forgiveness removes the barriers that would exist between God and man. Once man receives this forgiveness then the barriers on his part are removed and he is reconciled to God.

God knows all men have sinned and so His purpose is to reveal to man His reconciliation. Job needed to hear the message of what God could do and would do for him. These men made sin the big issue and it only brought Job into greater condemnation and frustration. They could have had the same revelation as Abraham, but they had more of religious knowledge than understanding of God's revelation. No one will grow in the Lord who has his eyes on sin more then on the righteousness that God gives to him. We will see that when his eyes were turned off from his being a sinner and unto the Lord, things began to change in his life. Only as the light was turned on did Job become conscious of his sins for we will see that Job repented.

Third step of their wrong view of God: God sees people as worthless.

Those men saw Job and all men as only evil. "No man can be righteous before God. No man born of women can be pure. Man is only a maggot and a worm in God's sight." Job 25:4–6. Job 15:14–16—"Man is only vile and corrupt and no one born of women can be righteous in His sight." Job 15:14-16 That was not only a false view of God and man, but it was a slap in God's face concerning His creation of man and His salvation to make man righteous.

Watch when religion places God so high that man can not be reconciled to Him. God made man in His image and it is God's purpose to redeem man to Him, to recreate him in His image and to walk and talk with man. In Ephesians 1:5, it is not only God's will but His very pleasure to redeem man. Though this is spoken in the New Testament, God never changes. It was His will and pleasure to redeem Abraham, Job, and all believers. God does not view man as these men did but He longs to reconcile man back into the image God created him.

During Jesus' ministry on this earth, the Jewish religious leaders would not use the name of God lest they take it in vain. They placed God so high that they didn't know what it meant to be made righteous in His sight. It was amazing that Jesus came not only speaking of God constantly, but referred to Him in a personal way as Father. He told all His followers to approach God this way. Jesus never spoke of God being so mighty that man cannot relate to Him, but just the opposite, Jesus always was bringing man into His Father's presence.

No believer should ever deny God's greatness. It was not these men's view of God being great was wrong; but their view that His greatness placed barriers between sinful man and a Holy God. This view keeps man out of God's presence. Yet this is the work of God's redemption for man that God has made a way for man to be restored in His Image and come into His presence.

Forth step of their wrong view of God: They failed to see God's purpose of man – Believers would be God's glorious family on this earth.

In creation God was so pleased to create man to be His family. Man would be able to experience all the blessings and love of God. God was pleased to call man His own. He then placed man on this earth to represent Him. Yet when Adam sinned this image of God in Adam was marred and his being God's representative was destroyed. God's salvation redeems man back into His family to be His representative on this earth. God is so pleased to have people who respond to Him and are His testimony on this earth. Our God is a restoring God. In Ezekiel 33:11—"declares the Sovereign Lord, I take no pleasure in the death of the wicked." Again in II Peter 3:9—"He (The Lord) is patient with you, not wanting anyone to perish, but everyone to come to repentance."

Man is of value because he was created in the image of God and then redeemed by the precious blood of the Son of God. The whole word of revelation is God redeeming man to Himself, bringing man into Sonship, and being able to fellowship with man. What a day it was when Jesus came to this earth. Here was One in God's image representing God on this earth. It says of Jesus that the Father "was pleased to have all His fullness dwell in Him"(His Son). Colossians.1:19 From Abraham until now, God is so pleased to redeem man back into His image and likeness and to reign on earth. This is what God says about us His Sons. "For the earnest expectation of the creation eagerly waits for the revealing of the Sons of God." Romans. 8:19

These men had a wrong knowledge of God and this is how they treated Job. How we see God is how we treat men. When one sees God's love to redeem man then we will treat others the same way. These men's view of God was He delights in condemning us – putting man down and counting him as nothing. Job let their view of God influence him and he never moved in faith the whole time those men spoke to him. We are not sure how long those men ministered to Job, but they never helped him. They only made him feel greater condemnation.

Fifth step of their wrong view of God. They failed to see God was a God of grace.

Peter refers to the Lord, "as the God of all grace." God never wanted man to experience the curse of sin. He has always wanted man to be reconciled to Himself. In Ezekiel 33:11, "As I live says the Lord God, I have no pleasure in the death of the wicked but that the wicked turn from his way and live." John 1:17 says "Grace and truth came by Jesus Christ." (NKJV) Grace is not just another doctrine to teach but it is the very life of Jesus. You cannot separate Jesus and grace. Jesus is grace. This is why the gospel is called the good news. It is glad tidings of good things. Romans.10:15 Job only heard from his friends sin and thatGod was not pleased with him.

God's Word says in Romans. 4:16 "it is of faith that it may be according to grace." (NKJV) Job's friends kept pointing to his sin and never the favor or grace of God. This kept Job in a position of trying to justify Himself. Once he began to hear God's favor, that God was not against him but for him then things begin to take a turn in his life. Trying to do better, taking all the good steps a believer ought to take will not give you victory. It is not what you do but what you believe about the Grace of God. In life it is not in what we do to be better but it is what we believe. How believers today need to hear the glorious message of God's grace. Our problem is that in the Covenant on Mt. Sinai there was an expectation to do the right thing and God will bless you. In the New Covenant Jesus has already done it for us and we need to believe. Grace is all what Jesus had done for us. The law of self-efforts is what we do and if it is what we do then it rules out grace.

Believers today have the revelation of Jesus and His grace. Yet, without realizing it they are still living under the Old Covenant of works and self-efforts. In the Old Covenant we are told if there is sin in our lives then the Lord won't hear us. If we bring these verses forth in our lives under the New Covenant, it leaves us in a state of trying to get right with God without trusting what He has already done for us. Under God's grace, He tells us" to come boldly to the throne of grace so we may obtain mercy and find grace to help in time of need." Hebrews. 4:16 (NKJV) If we have failures or sins then it is a time of need and God is not holding us at arms length until we have gotten everything right but we come into His grace so He can get things right for us. Even when we sin we are to come boldly, I John 2:1-2 says "If anyone sins we have an Advocate with the Father, Jesus Christ the righteous and He is the atoning sacrifice for our sins."(NKJV) It is being under the Covenant of Grace that we have access into His presence and this is our victory.

Here are some verses that speak of the grace of God as the only way to live a Christ like life.

> Rom. 5:17 "much more those who receive abundance of grace and of the gift of righteousness will reign in life through the One Jesus Christ." (NKJV) Grace enables us to Reign in Life.

> Rom. 5:20 "but where sin abounded, grace abounded much more." (NKJV) Grace is greater then sin.

> Rom. 6:14 "for sin shall not have dominion over you, for you are not under law but under grace." (NKJV) Grace gives us power over sin.

> Titus 2:11-12 "For the grace of God that brings salvation has appeared to all men teaching us that, denying ungodliness and worldly lust we should live soberly, righteously and Godly in the present age." (NKJV) Grace teaches us how to live Godly.

CHAPTER 9

Fourth Man, Elihu's
Counsel To Job

Now a fourth man entered into conversation with Job. His name was Elihu. He was younger than the other three. His age difference had kept him from speaking. It was because of Elihu's counsel that God was able to restore Job. There are some who see Elihu's counsel as the same as Eliphaz, Bildad, and Zophar. Yet it is clear in Job 42:7–9 that it was only those three men whom God said, "I am angry with you and your two friends because they have not spoken of Me what is right." Those three, and not Elihu, were to take a sacrifice to Job so that Job could pray for them.

Elihu's counsel shows us how God was able to reveal Himself to Job. Elihu's counsel turned Job's eyes off of himself and onto the Lord. It was through his counsel that Job began to see God's revelation that led to his restoration. How did Elihu approach Job. What did he say to Job. What was the results of his counsel.

STEPS IN COUNSELING:

These are basic steps in counseling and helping others through their difficulties. Elihu's counsel to Job sets forth the following fundamental steps in counseling.

1. All counseling must have a desire to restore; never to condemn.

Elihu's encounter with Job began in chapter 32. Elihu did not speak until the three other men had stopped speaking. He was younger and gave them the opportunity to say all that they wanted to say before he spoke. The Bible says he was angry with these men because **they condemned Job without giving him helpful counsel.** Satan had attacked Job and left him in a state of hopelessness. Instead of these men helping Job they poured more condemnation on him. Job didn't need to hear words of condemnation but how he could be restored. It is far easier to see the wrong in another than it is to help restore him.

In Galatians 6:1—"if a brother is caught in a sin, you who are spiritual should restore him gently." This is one of the few places in the Bible that it speaks of a spiritual person. A spiritual person is one who not only sees the wrong, but is able to gently help restore that person. The spiritual man is not one who only sees a failure, but he is willing to help that person in his failure. Watch when you condemn someone without being able or willing to help them. The three men seemed to want to prove Job wrong. Counseling is only effective when one's feelings toward the one being counseled are positive. That is why there is no condemnation in Christ because His whole work of reconciling man is positive. In John 3:17, it says that Jesus came not to condemn but restore. The very heart of our Heavenly Father is one of redemption, not condemnation.

The reason why Elihu's counsel was so powerful is he approached Job with the revelation of God's redemption of man. In any situation our focus must always be on restoration, never on condemnation. That set the stage in Elihu's approach to Job and how he would respond to Job. The bedrock foundation in counseling is to restore.

2 All counseling must be willing to wait, listen, and give full attention.

As Elihu began to speak, he mentioned three things that he did before he ever spoke.

- Job 32:4 and 11—He waited.
- Job 32:5-6,10-11—He listened:
- Job 32:12—He gave his full attention.

The other three men had kept talking and trying to prove Job wrong. But Elihu did not rush to speak. He waited and listened, he gave his full attention to what was being said. I must confess at times when I have been trying to help someone, I have developed an answer for them before they finish speaking. I have been more concerned to give them my answer than I was to listen and give them my full attention.

It seems that Jesus wanted to teach when He was 12. But His heavenly Father told Him to wait. It says He went to Nazareth with them (His earthly parents) and was obedient to them. Jesus, as man, was learning to wait, listen, and give his full attention to His Father's words and what was happening in the world around Him. It was Elihu's waiting, listening, and giving his full attention that led to some very powerful steps in helping Job with his recovery.

3. All counseling must rely on the Holy Spirit giving us God's revelation.

Elihu did not rely on his age or even his experience as much as he relied on the Holy Spirit.

Even though he was young yet he relied on the Spirit of God. Elihu gave way to their age and experience. Job 32:6–7—I am young in years…I thought age should speak…advanced years should teach wisdom. But Elihu trusted the Spirit of God.

Job 32:8—"but it is the Spirit in man, the breath of the Almighty, that gives him understanding." Job 33:4— "the Spirit of God has made me, the breath of the Almighty gives me life."

Elihu acknowledged the breath (which means Spirit) of God. He not only acknowledged the Spirit of God but testified that God's Spirit had given him understanding. His acknowledgement of the Spirit of God stood in contrast to how the other three had come to their understanding. Read through the speeches of the three men, you find that they relied on age and experience. Age and experience can be very powerful, if that life has walked with and relied on the Spirit of God. If it hasn't, then no matter the age or experience; their counsel will only be from the earthly realm and it will never bring forth God's life. Only by the Spirit of God can we receive God's revelation of how to live.

In Job 15:9–10, Eliphaz said, "What do you know that we do not know? What insights do you have that we do not have? The gray-haired and the aged are on our side, men even older than your father." Job 15:17–18—"Let me tell you what I have seen (his experience) what wise men have declared, hiding nothing received from their fathers."

Zophar said in Job 20:3–4—"my understanding inspires me to reply. Surely you know how it has been from of old, ever since man was placed on the earth."

Bildad said in Job 8:8–9—"ask the former generations and find out what their fathers learned. For we were born only yesterday and know nothing, and our days on earth are but a shadow. Will they not instruct you and tell you? Will they not bring forth words from their understanding?"

In the beginning of this study, we saw that there was a

world system and people were under it until they became believers. Once a person becomes a believer, they are under the reign of God (both Old and New Testament saints). It is the Holy Spirit who imparts God's revelation. God's revelation was the key to Job's situation and it is the key to any problem any believer may have. This is why all believers need the Spirit of God bringing His word of revelation.

It is thrilling to know that Jesus is called the Counselor. He is one who imparts God's ways to His people (See Isaiah 9:6.) Then Jesus spoke of sending the Holy Spirit, called the Counselor. In the Greek this word means "one called beside". You may say, "That is only for New Testament times". Yet, God has always revealed Himself to those who wanted to know Him and to walk with Him. Noah, Abraham, Isaac, Jacob, and Joseph all received God's revelation.

Yet Job's three friends, like so many today, have the attitude that we cannot really know God or His ways. Job 11:7 "Can you fathom the mysteries of God? Can you probe the limits of the Almighty?" This is completely contrary to God's revelation to Noah, Abraham, Isaac, Jacob, Joseph and Jesus' revelation to us. In fact, Jesus spoke of how we can know the Father and His ways. God's revelation in the Old Testament and Jesus' ministry in the New Testament were never to keep us in the dark about God, but to bring His revelation to us. He is a God who has always wanted to make Himself and His ways known to His people.

The three friends of Job relied on their own wisdom of

age and the experience of men who went before them and missed hearing what God wanted to say to them. Today there is a great emphasis on Christian counseling, but too often it is relying on one's qualifications and degrees instead of the ministry of the Holy Spirit. Much of modern day Christian counseling though well meaning relies more on psychology and human steps then on the revelation of our Lord Jesus Christ.

4. All counseling must have the attitude of identification.

Elihu approached Job with the attitude of I am just like you. His approach was not to bring more condemnation on Job, but to identify with him. Job 33:6–7—"I am just like you before God; I too have been taken from clay. No fear of me should alarm you, not should my hand be heavy upon you."

This was like a breath of fresh air to Job. This man knew God had dealt with him in a loving way and he was not going to approach Job in hardness and condemnation. Elihu knew he was taken from clay. That corresponds to II Corinthians 4:7—"we have this treasure in jars of clay." In other words, as human beings, our lives and emotions are very fragile. Most people would say "I am fragile please approach me and counsel me with care."

Jesus spoke of this in Matthew 7:3–5 about the speck in your brother's eye and a plank in your own. Jesus said take the plank out of your own eye and you will then see how to remove the speck from your brother's eye. Jesus used the eye as an example of removing foreign matter from it, as it is the most intricate operation; therefore, it needs to be handled with extreme care. Notice what Jesus was saying. It is after you have had an eye operation then you will be able to help your brother with his operation. Only after you have cleared your vision will you see clearly to operate on another.

We may not identify with others in the same sin or failure. But we can identify with our having had sinned and failed, and God in His love and grace operated on us. Paul's words to Titus in Titus 3:3–5—Titus don't forget what we were like, "at one time we too were foolish, disobedient, deceived and enslaved by all kinds of passions and pleasures. We lived in malice and envy being hated and hating one another. But when the **kindness and love of God our Savior appeared**, He saved us."

Paul was saying to Titus; don't forget what we were like and how God treated us. Now, Titus, you treat others the same way as we were treated. In the verse before this (Titus 3:2), Paul was encouraging him to be peaceable, considerate, and to show true humility toward all men. Paul knew by experience this was how God dealt with him and he is saying we need to approach others the same way. To respond any other way brings forth the fruit of condemnation.

Often we hear people say that we cannot help someone unless we have experienced the same failure, sin, or setback. Is this true? Here is what God revealed to me. When

I went into the jail on my first Bible Study, (I am now Chaplain) I knew most of the inmates had been on drugs. Drugs were not around when I was in high school – at least not in this area. Yet my sins and insecurities was just as great as theirs. God said, "Son, you go in love and teach them My words of victory." Then after many months God revealed to me that I didn't have to participate in drugs to help those on drugs. God revealed to me that Jesus was never on drugs and He has helped more drug-addicts then anyone else. He was never depressed yet He has healed many depressed people. He was never lustful but has delivered many men who have been led into pornography. Then many months later. God revealed to me that it is not that we have to experience the same sin to help someone but we must experience the same power of His Sacrifice to forgive and deliver us from sin. You don't have to experience the same sin but you do need to experience the same Grace of our Lord Jesus no matter what the sin may be. It was not that I was on drugs, but I was very insecure, I was rejected and struggled in school . I spent most of my time in the principal's office and this led me to do things that was just as bad as drugs. The same Lord Jesus that changed my life can change a drug addict. I may not have the same sin but I do have the same Savior. Beloved you may not be identified in the same sin but you are able to minister to them because you have experienced the same Redemption. Praise Jesus it is not the sin but the experience of Jesus in our lives.

The greatest identification was when the Lord Jesus

became man. He identified with us by experiencing on this earth all that we experience. He was hungry; tired; thirsty; weary; rejected, and tempted in the same way as all men are tempted. No wonder He was moved by compassion and love. No wonder He testified, "I have not come to bring more condemnation upon man for I have come to save him out of this wretched mess." Once mercy and restoration have been your experience, then you will have that desire of mercy and restoration for another. This was the fundamental difference in the counsel of Elihu and the other three men. This ought to be our prayer, "Lord, how can we approach others in helping them just as you have helped me?" He is a redeeming God and this aim is how we need to identify with others who are experiencing difficulties.

5. Any one being counseled needs to know there is a mediator on his/her behalf.

Elihu by revelation knew that man needs a mediator who stands between man and God. Job said in his answers to the three men, Job33:23–25—"Yet if there is an angel on his side as a mediator, one out of a thousand to tell a man what is right for him, to be gracious to him and say, 'Spare him from going down to the pit, I have found a ransom for him' then his flesh is renewed like a child's it is restored as in the days of his youth."

Even Abraham experienced Melchizedek, who was a priest, ministering on Abraham's behalf before God.

A mediator is someone who is on your side and can represent you to God. Elihu was speaking of a mediator before Christ was manifested or even before Aaron's earthly priesthood was established. In his spirit, he had the revelation of a mediator.

Job's desire was to go before God and prove his case. Yet in his inner spirit, he spoke of having a mediator in Job 16:19–21—"Even now my witness is in heaven; my ADVOCATE is on high. My INTERCESSOR is my friend as my eyes pour out tears to God; on behalf of a man, he pleads with God as a man pleads for his friend." It seems that though Job felt in his own spirit there could be a mediator, he didn't fully see the revelation of one. It was Elihu, under the inspiration of the Holy Spirit, who revealed to Job that there is the ministry of a mediator.

Satan attacked Job. His three friends condemned him. Society rejected him. Was there no one who was willing to go to God on his behalf? The only revelation he had was that the mediator could be an angel. Yet the good news to Job was that God was on his side and not against him. Job's experience was that everyone was against him. Wow! Someone who was from God was for me! He was one who was going to favor Job. The devil had already stolen from Job and he had received nothing but condemnation from his friends. Was it possible that God would favor Job? One who could speak into Job's life and see it restored? That was a message of hope to Job. Finally he was hearing good news. In Job 33:26 Elihu gives Job hope as he says, "He prays to God and finds favor with Him. He sees

God's face and shouts for joy. He is restored by God to his righteous state." Job finally felt that there was one who was on his side before God. This mediator was for Job and accepted him.

Elihu mentioned the results. He saw God's face. Job 33:26 (Always throughout Scripture seeing God's face was a revelation of Himself). In II Chronicles 7:14—"If my people who are called by my name will humble themselves and pray and seek my face…" and in II Corinthians 4:6—"to give us the light of the knowledge of the glory of God in the face of Christ.") This result means man can rejoice and shout praise to the Lord. He is restored. He realized his sin or consciousness of his wrongs. He had a glorious testimony. He had light that he could walk in. Elihu said to Job, this hope is for you, God is for you and His desire is that you can experience all of this.

In the New Testament, we know that Jesus is our mediator. He is for us and He will go to the Father on our behalf. Jesus' ministry is to intercede before the Father on our behalf. The glorious thing about Jesus as our mediator is that He loves to intercede for us and to restore all that the evil one has done to us. It is important that all counseling points to Jesus, the mediator. Once Job received the revelation of a mediator things began to change in his life.

6. All counseling will speak the truth to correct any wrongs.

God's counsel never overlooks any wrongs that have been committed. It always confronts man with the truth. There is a difference between condemnation and conviction. Satan comes to condemn man and this condemnation leaves him without any hope or salvation. God's purpose is not to condemn us in our wrong doing but to give us victory over it.

The very purpose of God's salvation is to redeem man from sin and to bring him into fellowship with God. Only when man is confronted with his sin can he then be forgiven and restored. This was how Elihu approached Job. It was after the first five counseling steps that he faced Job with the truth. The other three men condemned Job and left him without any hope of salvation. Condemnation not only tells us we are guilty, but piles the guilt on without any forgiveness. When counsel is built on grace, then it never has to shy away from confronting man with the truth.

Job's wrong was more in his attitude than in his actions. Elihu felt that Job was justifying himself rather than God. (Job 32:2) Read through what Job said, Job 13:3—"but I desire to speak to the Almighty and to argue my case with God." God's own words to Job were the same. Job 40:2—"Will the one who contends with the Almighty correct Him. Let him who accuses God answer Him." As long as Job tried to justify himself, he would never see victory in his life. This was the truth that Elihu brought before Job. Elihu approached Job with an attitude of seeing Job reconciled to God. Because reconciliation was his goal, he faced Job with the truth. Job, a man of God, was not afraid of the truth. In fact, when Job realized God was for him, he wanted to hear the truth.

Elihu confronted Job with the light. Elihu quoted what he heard Job say, Job 34:5—"I am innocent, but God denies me justice." In Job 34:9—"for he says it profits a man nothing when he tries to please God." Elihu said to Job, in Job 34:35—"Job speaks without knowledge; his words lack insight." Job felt he needed to justify himself in God's sight. If he or anyone else could justify themselves, then it would be their own works and efforts and not the grace of God.

God's Word is truth and it is light to our lives. When the light is turned on, then we are able to see areas in our lives that need to change. Dwelling on sin or condemning man in sin never turns the light on—only the truth of God's revelation is light. Job needed to come into the light. That was the only way for him to experience victory. Repentance without coming into the light will not bring forth a Godly life. True repentance comes when one comes into the light and the light reveals the glory and goodness of God. God is not just concerned that we try to leave sin but that we come into His Light and that light will cause us to leave sin and have victory over it.

7. All counseling must turn eyes off from self and onto the Lord to hear from Him.

All that Elihu was speaking to Job was to lead him to hear what God had to say. Elihu turned Job's eyes off of himself and unto the Lord to hear from God. It was after Elihu spoke to Job that Job was able to hear from God. His eyes were no longer on himself and he had ears to hear from God.

Two very significant things resulted after Elihu spoke to Job. First, Job no longer tried to justify himself. In fact, he never answered Elihu as he did the other three. Second, in Job 38:1 it says God began to speak to Job. This was the crowning point in Job's recovery. All Elihu's counsel led to the very moment that Job heard from God. The key to victory in any situation is that one turns His eyes off of himself to hear what God is saying. Often a believer has a problem and he says I have prayed over it. I have asked others to pray with me but there seems to be no answer. Though prayer is good and right, if the one praying never hears from the Lord, never turns to the Lord to hear what God is saying his prayers will not be effective. When ones hears from God then his prayers will be a joy and bring the answers. What is God saying to me in all of this? What does His Word say? I need to hear from Him.

CHAPTER 10

Job hears the Word of the Lord.

This is the goal of all counseling. Job needed to hear what God was saying. In Isaiah 55:8–9 it says God's thoughts are not our thoughts, therefore our ways are not His ways. We need to have God's thoughts on the things we face so we can respond to His way. Job needed God's view on his situation and that could only come by His Word. Job heard many voices and words but failed to hear what God wanted to reveal to him. As long as he failed to hear God's Word, things stayed the same in his life. When he realized he needed to hear what God wanted to say to him, then things began to change.

It is no different today. Many believers have all sorts of attacks and problems, but never hear what God is saying. Like Job, they focus on the attacks and they talk the problem without hearing what God wants to say to them. In their prayers, they speak the problem and tell God all about it. Instead of praying, "Lord you know what I am facing now, what do you want to say to me? Holy Spirit, I know you can impart to me the revelation that I need, so I come to listen and learn from you."

Job's three friends never pointed Job in that direction. They were not hearing from the Lord, so how could they tell Job to receive God's revelation? During those attacks, Job was not receiving God's revelation. Therefore, he had no knowledge into his problem. Like Job, many people want to see their problem solved, but they do not have ears to hear what God is saying. They want an answer, but neglect in receiving revelation. In any situation, the first thing we need to pray and seek is what God says about it. Many believers pray asking God to do something and then they say, "If it be your will." The only way any believer can know the will of God is through His Word and that word becoming revelation to us. It is not our pleading and crying out that brings the answers but what God is saying. Once we know what God is saying, then we can pray in faith.

From his experience, Job learned that counsel from his friends without God's Word was vain. His own opinions failed him. Pleading with God brought no answer. It was amazing how long that went on in Job's life with his eyes cast on himself and pleading with God to hear him. It wasn't that God didn't hear him, but <u>God wanted Job to hear from Him.</u>

Some may say Job didn't have as much revelation as we do today. Believers today have the complete Word of God. Yes, that is very true. Yet we are never to limit God's revelation to his people. Noah had God's revelation in fulfilling God's purpose and will for his life. Abraham had God's full revelation of all that God called him to be and do. Job had God's revelation as God testifies to it. Then we saw how Elihu had God's revelation to help Job. Man misses God's revelation; not because God has not given it, but that man fails to receive it..

I have heard people quote I Peter 5:7—"casting all your care on Him for He cares for you." (NKJV) After they quote this, they then say, "Don't go and pick it up again." I want to tell you that unless you hear what God is saying about your problem, you won't know how to cast the problem onto the Lord. You may try to give it to the Lord, but it will remain with you until you hear from God and believe what He says. When His Word becomes more powerful than your cares, then you will experience casting it all on Him and having victory. This is why we read in the Scriptures over and over, "God spoke" or "God spoke through a prophet". The key is God speaking His Word into a believer's life and situation. How can anyone ever live God's life without hearing His Word? Even Jesus, the very Son of God, testified that man cannot live by bread alone but by the very Word of God.

Good principles will help us to live a better life, but to walk and talk with our Lord we need His daily revelation. The Word of God sets forth principles for living God's life. However, I see so many believers trying to condition themselves to live the principles, but not having God's living, active revelation. God's principles are a guide but His revelation is His life to us.

Satan attacks the Word of God more than anything else in our lives. Jesus testified to this in His teaching on the parable of the sower. The seed is the Word of God and it is the very thing that Satan comes and tries to take away from our lives. Then Jesus gave this interpretation in Mark 4:17, "When trouble or persecution comes **because of the word** they quickly fall away." Jesus said, "Because of the Word." Satan knows the power of the Word of God in a life. He does not mind us praying, as long as we are not praying the Word. He does not mind us going to church services, as long as the Word of God is not effective in our lives. But once we receive the Word, then that is what He attacks. It was his first attack on Eve, Satan tried to bring doubt to Eve by asking her, "Did God really say…" Genesis 3:1. Satan knows the only way we can live God's life on this earth and fulfill His creation purpose is by the Word of God. No wonder, the Lord says four times in the Bible, "the just shall live by faith."

It is the same with many believers today. Things happen in their lives and they keep on pleading and crying out to God. They even get others to pray for them, yet fail to hear what God is saying to them. It is not a question of why is this happening to me, but what is God saying to me in this situation? This was the key to Job's restoration and it has always been the key for all believers.

Do you see why it was important for Job to hear from God? Do you have a better understanding of why he failed to have victory. Job kept justifying himself without hearing what God wanted to say to him? Hearing the Word of God was Job's answer to his suffering. It was not sitting back and saying, "Why do the Godly suffer?" and "May the Lord be praised because of it." Our outlook ought to be I can hear from God and He will reveal to me His Living Word.

Seven Reasons Why the Word is so Vital to Our Lives

First, it is only by His Word that we can live His life on this earth. Job didn't need to live under Satan's reign nor does any believer. As believers, we can live His life because God has given us His Word.

Second, only the Word can give us the knowledge of God. God's revelation is not given to us through trials, suffering, or any other natural earthly realm. God's Word is His knowledge and He has given us His Word so we can know Him and His ways.

Third, His Word is His daily revelation to us. It is from His revelation of His Word that we can commune and live in a relationship with Him. Our prayer life ought to be a two-way street. This means we not only talk to God, but we learn to listen and hear from Him.

Fourth, God's Word of revelation to us reveals and exposes the enemy's attacks upon our lives. The more sensitive we are to God's life through His Word, the more we will discern the enemy and his ways. You will only discern the enemy by coming into the Light of God's Word.

Fifth, God's Word is what builds our shield of faith so that we can overcome all the works of the evil one. Ephesians 6:16 and Romans. 10:17

Sixth, God's Word is not just for a quick fix, but is to establish our lives in God.

Seventh, It is only through God's Word that we have the revelation of who we are as God's people and all with which God wants to bless us . This was revealed to Abraham and on down to believers today. God has always wanted to bless His people and let them know how special they are. Job had this revelation and God's protection, but he failed to live in God's revelation when the attacks began.

Do you recall that Jesus didn't say the truth will set you free? But He said you will *know* the truth and then you will be set free. It was the revelation of God that set Job free and it will be the only thing that will set any believer free. It was not Job's pleading and crying out to God, but he needed to hear the truth.

CHAPTER 11

God's Word to Job

Elihu gave Job hope when he said to him, "For God does speak, now one way and now another." God's Word was what Job needed. No wonder God spoke to Isaiah the words, "For My (God) thoughts are not your thoughts; neither are your ways My ways." In Isaiah 55:8, Isaiah then spoke of the Word of God and in verse11—"so is My word that goes out from my mouth." This is what Job heard, the Word of God. Job 38:1 "Then the Lord answered Job out of the whirlwind and said," (NKJV) He was speaking to Job. How can Job or any believer ever live God's life without hearing from God?

Finally Job heard what God was saying to him. The very first thing God said to Job concerning His Word. Job 38:2—"Who is this that darkens My counsel with words without knowledge?" This was what made Elihu's counsel so effective. He was pointing Job in the direction of hearing from God. Elihu had said the same thing as God did to Job. Job 34:35—"Job speaks without knowledge, his words lack insight." Job 35:16—"so Job opens his mouth with empty talk, without knowledge he multiplies words."

God is the one who said Job lacked knowledge; thereby praising God for what Satan had done to him. This shows why it was important for Job to hear from God. Someone said it is not that believers are doing a lot of wrong things as much as they lack knowledge in doing the right things. God was not saying that Job didn't have knowledge, but that he lacked having God's knowledge. It is only through the Word of God that believers can have the knowledge of God.

→ **After first attack**. Job 1:21—"The Lord gave and the Lord has taken away; may the name of the Lord be praised." Job saw these things as God's attacks and confessed it. It was under this confession that his attacks continued. This is Job speaking and God says he lacked the knowledge of God. How often have believers heard this verse quoted without realizing what God says they are words without knowledge. Yes the Lord did bless Job but it was not the Lord who killed his children. John 10:10 makes it clear that God is not the thief or the destroyer.

→**After God spoke to Job**. Job 40:3–5—"Then Job answered the Lord. I am unworthy – how can I reply to you? I put my hand over my mouth, I spoke once, but I have no answer, twice, but I will say no more."

Again God spoke to Job. God was not finished with His revelation to Job. It was not that God was trying to condemn Job, but God had greater things for Job to experience; however, he was not going to receive them until He knew what God wanted to say to him. The greater the light, the greater our faith can grow to receive and be what God has called us to be. To put it in human terms, God was saying to Job, "Job I am not finished with you, I have so much more for you to experience of all my love and goodness to you. You are my glorious representative to reveal My life to those around you."

Job had nothing to say. He was seeing things from God's perspective and he ceased to use his own human logic. God said to Job in Job 40:8—"Would you discredit my justice? Would you condemn Me to justify yourself?" God's purpose was not to condemn Job, but to see his full restoration. It is God's revelation that brings the light and it is only by the light that sin can be revealed. God, by His revelation, was bringing to light things in Job's life to set him free. God never pointed out any man's sin to condemn him but always to bring him into the light. As God brings Job into the light then Job sees his sins and failures and seeks God for forgiveness. God's heart is always to restore man and to bring him into His abundance.

God had Job's attention and was speaking into his life. God's revelation was not just a quick fix to overcoming his problem, but that the life of God might be established in Job. The Word of God is not given just for a quick fix (sometimes it may be necessary), but rather to teach us how to trust our God and live His life in this world. This means that it was not just what God was saying to Job at this time, but God wanted Job to walk and talk with

Him daily. Job had heard from God, and then somehow he stopped hearing and began to be led by things in the natural human realm. We know that after his first attack Job spoke part of the Word of God ("the Lord gave") but also spoke his own opinion ("the Lord has taken away"). It seems that his opinion had more influence on him than the word of revelation. God's revelation to His people is always a continuous ministry.

God was turning His light on in Job's life. It was the light of His revelation to Job that revealed His love and goodness to him and brought to the surface Job's real condition. Repentance can only come as the light is turned on in a life. This is why many believers stay on the same tread mill of confession as they constantly ask God to forgive them of their sins without ever receiving the light of His Word. Job had no problem seeing his sin once he received the light of God's Word.

This was the glorious moment of Job's experience. God was speaking to him personally. When all others had cast him aside and then condemned him, God stepped in with His Word. That reassured Job that God was still for him. God was bringing some things to the surface, but He was speaking to Job. Job understood that God still loved him, and he was once again hearing God's voice to him.

God speaks of Satan's power

God then began to speak to Job about two animals, the behemoth and the leviathan. This is the only place that behemoth is mentioned. The Leviathan is mentioned twice, in the Psalms and in Isaiah 27:1. As you read of these two animals Job 40:15 and Job 41:34, the description given is not speaking of an earthly animal.

Behemoth – He ranks first among the works of God. No one can capture him.

Leviathan – Job 41:3 "Will he keep begging you for mercy? Will he speak to you with gentle words? Job 41:5— Can you tame him as a pet? Job 41:8 "If you lay a hand on him, you will remember the struggle and never do it again." Job 41:11—"Everything under heaven belongs to me." Job 41:25—"When he rises up the mighty are terrified." Job 41:33—"Nothing on earth is his equal – a creature without fear." Job 41:34—"He is king over all that are proud. Also in Isaiah 27:1—"leviathan the gliding serpent, leviathan the coiling serpent."

What is said about these two animal creatures seems to be speaking about more than just physical, earthly creatures. In Ezekiel 28:11–19 it speaks of the King of Tyre. The language used was not just referring to an earthly king, but also to a greater being. There is no doubt that it was speaking of Satan and his life. Satan is a spirit and therefore cannot be seen. So God describes him in language we can understand.

The same thing is true in Isaiah 14:12–17. God is describing Satan so that we can understand his being and life. In Psalm 91:13—"You will tread upon the lion and the cobra; you will trample the great lion and the serpent." This also refers to satanic powers and demons. God's word to Job about these two animals, and especially the leviathan, was describing more than just an animal creature. There seems to be little doubt that God was revealing to Job the presence and power of Satan.

We have no indication that Job knew these attacks were by Satan. God was telling Job these forces of evil were way beyond his control. He is king and you cannot tame him. Job 41:9 (NKJV) "Indeed, any hope of overcoming him is false; shall one not be overwhelmed at the sight of him." This was the battle Job was encountering. It is true that no man can tame or control the evil one, anymore than you can tame and control sin. In fact God knew man could not tame Satan. God was revealing to Job the battle was far greater than his own understanding or his own resources. His battle was one with leviathan the serpent, Satan himself.

Without God's intervention there was no way that Job could overcome the attacks of Satan. The attacks on Job and also on believers are not just in the physical earthly realm there is a greater source behind them. God was revealing to Job the depth and power of these attacks? Even Jesus never tried to tame Satan. He came to destroy him and take dominion over him. Job's battle was seen in the natural realm but the source of it was from the spirit realm of evil forces.

Scripture is clear that Job was not just fighting flesh and blood or natural events. That battle was far greater than what met Job's natural eye. He needed God's revelation that brings the light to expose the evil one. Satan is only exposed by the light of God's revelation. No natural means ever exposes Satan. He is only exposed or detected by the light.

Jesus' life and ministry is a powerful example of Satan being detected as the source of all evil events. Why was Satan mentioned so much during Jesus' ministry? Surely he didn't just come on the scene at the time of Jesus. Satan has always been active in this world. It was that he was exposed during the time of Jesus' ministry. It was not that he was not active before then, but he was able to hide and people never realized his ministry. Satan will always be undetected when there is no spiritual light. The reason Satan was not able to hide from Jesus is that Jesus is the pure light from His Father. Satan can't stand the light because it exposes him. Only the light brings Satan to the surface and all his evil acts. Jesus saw Satan as the source of all evil and wrongs, such as peoples' illnesses, the blindness of religious leaders, attacking Jesus and entering Judas. Twice Jesus spoke of Satan as the source in Peter's life. Read through the gospels and mark down every time it mentions Satan or evil spirits. They could never hide from Jesus—His life always brought them to the surface and exposed them.

We never read that Jesus said His Father was permitting Satan to attack people. In fact, we read that He came to destroy Satan's work, not to give Satan His approval. Jesus didn't give Satan permission to attack Peter, just the opposite, "Peter I am praying for you during this attack." Read about Jesus' attitude toward Satan and his works in Mark 1:27—"With authority He even gave orders to evil spirits and they obeyed Him." Two of the main things Jesus spoke to evil spirits were, "shut up" and "get out."

Jesus came to minister His Father's life to a fallen world and He never came to give Satan permission to attack His people. In fact, He used His authority as a means to detect and then defeat Satan. Jesus Himself testified to the fact that He had power over evil forces by the Holy Spirit. (Read Matthew 12:28.) The reason believers are not sensitive to Satan's work is that they are not sensitive to the ministry of the Holy Spirit and the revelation of His Word. It is not just head knowledge of the Bible, but it is the living active Word in our lives. In John's gospel it mentions the Word becoming flesh in Jesus' life, and it is the same with us His followers.

Believers love to quote the verses in Ephesians 6:10–18—"For our struggle is not against flesh and blood... against the spiritual forces of evil in the heavenly realms." Let me illustrate something I remember saying to my wife when I came home from my office one day. I said, "You know believers quote 'For we do not fight against flesh and blood but the forces of evil'. But do you know that if a believer has a problem at work or in his family with another person, his focus is on that person and never realizing Satan is behind it?"

How did Jesus detect Satan? Jesus knew He was His Father's representative on the earth. Even though He was living in the physical realm, He realized that He was living from the heavenly realm. That means He was living His life on this earth from heaven's view point. If He was living heaven's life on this earth, then He needed to experience the anointing of the Holy Spirit and the revelation of His Father. This exposed Satan and brought him out into the light.

What God was saying to Job in chapters 38–41? God did not tell Job what to do to become a better believer. In His Word to Job, God spoke of His creative power and greatness, His righteousness, the realm of man (the natural), and the realm of God (the heavenly). God enlightened Job to the forces of evil that man cannot control. He never told Job what he needed to do in his daily life to be more committed to God. This is a powerful key in our walk of faith. Job's faith didn't need to be in what he needed to do, but in what God is able to do. No one will move in faith by being told what to do as a believer. Many believers are constantly told what to do but never have the revelation of what God can do in their daily lives. They lack the revelation of Christ and His daily provision for them; yet they keep hearing the same thing about being more committed to the Lord. Of course, at times we need to be told what to do! But that is not the foundation of our walk with the Lord.

In Ephesians 6:10–20, there is a very good example that emphasizes this. I have asked believers what portion of Ephesians they have heard the most sermons and teachings on. They have said that they have heard more sermons on Ephians. 6, the armor of God than on any other portion in Ephesians. Yet in the first 3 chapters of

Ephesians, nothing is said about what believers must do; but rather all that God has done for us through Christ Jesus. Yet much preaching zeros in on putting on the armor of God and misses the solid revelation in chapters 1-4. These chapters zero in on, 1) Who we are in Christ, 2) What we have in Christ, and 3) What we are able to do in Christ. Do you realize in the book of Ephesians it mentions our life is in the heavenly realms, our blessings are in the heavenly realms, and our battle is in the heavenly realms? It is not just hearing it once but the more we receive the more there is for us. This is what builds our faith to hear what God has done and what it means to me as a believer.

Paul's writing to the saints to put the armor comes at the end of his letter. If you go to Ephesians 1:18, Paul prayed that their eyes would be open. He was not praying for them to be faithful in battle, but to see what they have in Christ and what it means to them. Praise God we live in a time when God has done everything He needs to do! We are the ones who need our eyes open to see. Unless we have our eyes open to see who we are in Christ and what we have in Him, then how can we put on His armor?

Paul built their faith in the first three chapters of Ephesians and after that he tells them what to do. The same thing is true in Romans 12, telling believers to be a living sacrifice; yet chapters 2-8 tells us what God has done for us and what it means to us. After the first 11 chapters of Romans does he tell them to be a living sacrifice? Unless one's faith is built on what God has done and what it means to our lives, it is no use telling them what they must do.

Listen to many sermons and they center on what one must do. This is why many believers do not know how to live from the heavenly realm. First Paul took the time to build their faith in being God's representative, then he told them to go forth in the battle with all the armor. The armor was what he taught them after the first four chapters; then they would know how to put it on. The Lord was speaking the same thing to Job, it is not what you do but what you can believe about Me. God knew that if Job believed the right thing then he would live it. People live what they believe. Much of the emphasis today is do and then you will believe; but God's way is to believe and then you will do.

CHAPTER 12

Job's Response to God

It was what Job feared that brought these attacks. Satan works through our lives with fear as just the same as lust, greed or pride. God had so much more for Job to experience but He could not receive it with fear in his life. Instead of saying why do the Godly suffer we ought to say what is holding back the blessings of God. Once Satan attacked Job's fears, Job did not respond in faith over these attacks. Then Satan was able to use these three men to pour condemnation on Job and this dug him in deeper into self-pity. God did restore Job to a greater degree of blessings and faith. No longer would he let these fears control his life but the very revelation of God.

Job's testimony, "my ear had heard of you but now my eyes have seen you." I see things I never realized. I am hearing things that I didn't know. Though Job was a man who walked with the Lord, there were greater steps of faith that God was calling him to. The beauty of Job's life is that God had so much more for him to experience. The more glory and blessings that God bestowed on Job's life, the greater his testimony of the Lord became. God was not trying to make things difficult for Job but to open his eyes to see all the fullness he could experience.

Once again God gave Job an opportunity for him to respond to God's Word. His testimony was, "my ears had heard of you but now my eyes have seen you. Therefore I despise myself and repent in dust and ashes." Job 42:5–6 Job's response to the Lord was repentance. Do you recall that John the Baptist's message was repent and prepare the way of the Lord? All of Job's self-justification and trying to bargain with God was wrong. He realized that and asked God to forgive him. His repentance was not an end in itself but only preparing him for all that God wanted to do in his life. Job's repentance opened his life to receive from the Lord. Repentance is never an ends in itself but a step to turn us from sin to faith in our Lord Jesus Christ.

Many believers have experienced repentance only to do the same sin again. They repeat the same sin and confession. What did Job experience in his repentance that gave him the victory. Job repented once he came into God's light. He received God's revelation and he believed what God revealed to him. True repentance is not just what we come out of, but what God is bringing us into. Many believers are sincere and they know something is wrong and want to turn from it but they fail to receive God's revelation. What gives repentance strength is what God brings us into. If we are trying to have faith in our repentance then it becomes our works and man's works will always fail. If we come into God's revelation then we are believing what He has for us. The more we receive the light the greater will be the leaving of our sin. God never said the 'just shall live by repentance' but the 'just shall live by faith'. The more we come into the light of God's glory the greater will be our faith. Here are some examples from Scripture that their faith was the backbone to their repentance.

Jacob was a man who cheated his brother and deceived his father with lies. He had to leave his family because his brother threatened to kill him. That first night alone while he slept he had a dream. God never mentioned his sins of cheating or lying but God did reveal His light to Jacob. "Jacob this is what I have for you." Jacob believed the Lord and repentance was activated in his life. Read Genesis. 28:12-22.

Isaiah went up to the Temple to worship the Lord. He saw the glory of Jesus. John 12:41. It is then he repents and confesses, "I am a man of unclean lips and I live in the midst of men with unclean lips for my eyes have seen the King, the Lord of host." Isaiah 6:5 His repentance was backed by his receiving God's light. He not only turned from a man of unclean lips but believed what God had for him.

Peter is an example of the light being given that enables us to turn from our sins. Luke 5 tells of seeing two boats sitting at the water's edge while the fisherman were busy washing their nets, having caught nothing all night. Jesus entered one of the boats and asked Peter to put out a short ways from the shore. From there Jesus taught the people. When He had finished the men were ready to go home. However, Jesus told them to put out to sea and let down their nets. Because Jesus had asked them they did. Their nets became so full of fish that their boats began to sink. It was then that Peter fell on his knees and confessed, "I am a sinful man." Jesus never mentioned any sin but Peter's revelation of Jesus and His goodness empowered him to turn from his sin.

Once again God gave Job an opportunity for him to respond to God's Word. His testimony was, "my ears had heard of you but now my eyes have seen you. Therefore I despise myself and repent in dust and ashes." Job 42:5-6 The light brought Job to true repentance. Job's response to the Lord was repentance. All of Job's self-justification and trying to bargain with God was wrong. He realized that and asked God to forgive him. His repentance was not an end in itself, but only preparing him for all that God wanted to do in his life. Job's repentance opened his life to receive from the Lord. Repentance is never an ends in itself but a step to turn us from sin to faith in our Lord Jesus Christ.

After this, God spoke to Job about his human words lacking knowledge, He said to Job, "brace yourself like a man: I will question you and you shall answer Me." Job 40:7 God gave Job the opportunity he has asked for, to be able to come into God's presence and present his case Job 40:2–4. God went on and said, "Will the one who contends with the Almighty correct Him? Let him who accuses God answer Him." What was Job's answer to the Lord? "I am unworthy. How can I reply to you? I put my hand over my mouth. I spoke once, but I have no answer, twice, but I will say no more."

God's purpose was to bring these things to the surface in Job's life so he could be restored and brought into God's fullness. God could not build a solid relationship with Job if those things were not removed. No longer was Job asking God the question, "Why?" Like Job, believers will ask the question why, until they hear from the Lord. Once we hear from God, the question why is not as important as our hearing. Job's ears were attentive to what God was saying to him. His asking why, his self justification, his pleading and crying, all of those things faded as he heard God's revelation to him.

We can see Job's response to those attacks by Satan and his response to the Word of God. His response to Satan's attacks led him to confess negative things. But after hearing from the Lord, Job confessed in Job 40:4–5—"I put my hand over my mouth. I spoke once but I have no answer—twice, but I will say no more." Job 42:5—"My ears had heard of you but now my eyes have seen you." He is no longer confessing all the negative things that Satan was speaking into his life.

Our confession is very important in our walk of faith. Remember faith is believing what God has said. The word confession in the Greek is homologeo: there are two parts to this word: "homos", which means 'the same' and "leg", which means' to speak'. Therefore, confession means to speak the same thing. For example, we confess Jesus is Lord. We are speaking the very same thing that heaven speaks. We are agreeing with our Heavenly Father.

Job is like a lot of believers who are confessing what Satan says more than confessing what God says. Job confessed that the attacks were from God. He confessed that the day of his birth was a curse. He confessed that God was doing those things to him. Job was hearing more of Satan's words to him than God's words. Once He heard God speak then he could confess what God says.

Words have creative power. In Genesis 1 we read 11 times, "And God spoke," This is why the first step in receiving salvation is confessing with our mouth. In Romans 10:9–10, three times it mentions believing in our hearts and confessing with our mouths. These verses are saying our confession is as important as our believing. In fact, confession is part of our exercise of faith. Many in the body of Christ do not realize the power of their words and as a result, they talk illnesses, hard times, and problems but talk very little about the Word of God. In *Christ the Healer*, Bosworth said, "Wrong confession shuts the Father out and lets Satan in. We are to refuse to have anything to do with wrong confessions. When we realize that we will never rise above our confession, we are getting to the place where God can use us."

Job heard God's Word of revelation to him. He was no longer confessing Satan's negative thoughts and ways. Job was responding in faith, and as it says in I John 5:4—"This is the victory that has over come the world, even our faith." In every situation or attack of the enemy, hear what God says about it, then believe it in your heart, and confess it with your mouth. Stop confessing what Satan is saying.

It was Job, who finally realized that he could do something about his situation. Job didn't need to live under those attacks any longer. When believers mistakenly see these attacks as the will of God, they see them as inevitable in their lives. They pray and 'leave them with the Lord'. This breeds an attitude that this is of God and there is nothing we can do about it. It was not God who needed to take the steps but the man Job needed to see the God he served could cleanse and forgive, deliver him from his fears and overcome the attacks of the evil one.. Once he did, then things began to change.

.

Job's restoration didn't begin with everything being restored at once but began when he first heard God's Word to him and began to move forward. He had ears to hear and it led to his repentance and then receiving from the Lord. When he first heard the word of the Lord he didn't see any manifestation of his restoration but it had begun. Once any believer hears God's Word and responds to it then restoration is under way. Don't get upset if you do not see the manifestation of it. Be assured it is in process.

CHAPTER 13

God's Instruction to Job

First God told Job's three friends that he was not pleased with them. Even though they claimed to be speaking on God's behalf, they were not speaking what God spoke. They were to take a sacrifice and go to Job and he would pray for them. The three friends were willing to obey God and go to Job with a sacrifice. God was not just trying to prove those men wrong, but to see them restored. Ever since the fall of man, God's intention is to see men experiencing the blessings and life of God. No matter how wrong they were, God's desire was to see these men restored into fellowship with Him.

God wanted these men to be blessed as much as Job was blessed.

God knew Job's feelings toward these men. Job revealed his feelings by what he had said about these men. Job 12:3—"But I have a mind as well as you, I am not inferior to you." In Job 13:4—"You however, smear me with lies, you are worthless physicians, all of you." In Job 16:2—"I have heard many things like these, miserable comforters are you all." And in Job 16:11—"God has turned me over to evil men and thrown me into the clutches of the wicked." Job referred to them as miserable comforters. No matter how wrong those men were it does not give Job an excuse to have unforgiveness. His praying for them was a willingness to forgive them. However, Job could have refused to pray for them. After all, they had condemned Job. God was asking Job to forgive them.

Why was it important for Job to forgive them? Why does the Word of God say so much about forgiveness?

Unforgiveness hurts us more then the person who came against us. This leads to bitterness. This bitterness gives Satan an opportunity to use the situation. Our bitterness is Satan's work in our lives. It is bad enough for Satan to work in a life when one is hurt, but don't give him an opportunity to work in your life through unforgiveness. Forgiveness is heavens life, this is why Jesus, being crucified, cried out, "Father forgive them." Satan was the source of those men putting him to death, but Jesus was not going to let Satan work in His life. Two thousand years ago God took care of the sin problem and He has already forgiven the sins of everyone. Yet man must receive this forgiveness as this is God's gift of Salvation to man. God has never wanted sin to be barrier between Himself and man That is why God has always made provision for the atonement fir sin. If God forgives us, then we, his people, need to forgive.

It says in Ephesians that God was in Christ forgiving the world. This means whenever we are hurt and forgive, we are agreeing with God. If we do not forgive, then we are agreeing with the enemy. Once you agree with the enemy, you give him an opportunity to work. Satan is working through one life, why should I give him an opening in my life? I would rather agree with heaven and our Father than the devil. Job was God's representative and so he was responding to his situation the same way as God responded to him.

It was after Job prayed for his three friends that it says God made him prosper again. God forgave Job and Job in turn forgave his three friends. Job's relationship to the Lord was restored when He was forgiven and then his relationship to those three men was restored when he forgave them. It was a great day not only for Job but for his three friends as they all experienced the grace of God.

Job 42:11 speaks of Job's relatives. It says "they comforted and consoled him over all the trouble the Lord brought upon him." This was their own thoughts, but Job knew differently. He knew God was good and that God was not the one who brought those attacks; but rather Leviathan, the great serpent. God is the reconciler; the restorer, the One who removes the curse and brings the blessing.

After his restoration, Job had seven sons and three daughters. His daughters were given an inheritance with his sons. Job lived 140 years after the attacks by Satan. He lived long enough to see his fourth generation. Job had learned to walk in faith for his children and not in fear. The last thing said about Job was he died old and full of years. It is saying he received the Lord's goodness and lived it out in his life.

CONCLUSION

Job didn't understand why these things were happening to him. Plus his three friends kept feeding him with guilt and condemnation. It is important we do not condemn ourselves. It is bad enough to be attacked by the enemy and he then brings us under guilt and condemnation. Condemnation is never from the Lord even when we fail or sin God does not condemn us. This is the glorious power of God's forgiveness. As we see Him, He forgives and restores us. God's ministry to Job was not to focus on why these things happened to him but on his relationship with the Lord. Our focus on our past will never enable us to experience what God has for us today.

Then how should we respond to things that take place in our lives that we do not understand? First, never lose sight that God loves you and you are very special to the Lord. Job never heard this from his three friends. He only heard how he had failed and because of his failure these things were happening to him. Second, instead of focusing on the past, be open to hear what God is saying to you at this present time. Once Job's eyes were turned unto the

Lord then God could minister to Job. God has always called His people to move in the light. The more we move in God's light we will be enabled to see our lives from God's view point.

Abraham is our example of God restoring man to his creation purpose. The very first thing God said to Abraham was all about being blessed. The Lord told Abraham, "I will bless you." "You will be a blessing." And "All peoples on earth will be blessed through you." Genesis 12:2-3 Abraham is called the Father of all believers.

At the end of his life, it says in Genesis 24:1—"Abraham was now old and advanced in years and the Lord had blessed him in every way." If you follow Abraham's decedents, Isaac, Jacob, Joseph, and the nation of Israel, you will see that God, in His salvation, brought them under His blessing. It says in Numbers 6:22–27—"The Lord said to Moses, tell Aaron and his sons this is how you are to bless the Israelites:

> The Lord bless you and keep you.
>
> The Lord make His face shine upon you and be gracious to you,
>
> The Lord turn His face toward you and give you peace.
>
> So they will put my name on the Israelites and I will bless them."

In Deuteronomy 28, God set before the nation of Israel

blessings and cursings. They could choose to live under God's blessing or the curses. Job knew what it was to live under God's blessing and he also experienced the curse. God's purpose or will was not fulfilled in Job's attacks, but bringing him back under the blessing. The reason God gave us the revelation of Job's life was to exhort us to understand God's purpose in creating man to be blessed. His life was not set before us to see defeat and disaster in our lives as the will of our Father, but as the work of the enemy. Just ask the question,'who is the source of the blessing and who is the source of the curse?'. Satan must bear the full responsibility as the instigator of Job's disasters. Those attacks were totally from Satan and his curse. When we realize it is Satan who has done this, then we too, like Job will no longer be sitting back and saying "the Lord gives and the Lord takes away, may the name of the Lord be praised."

Job heard the word of the Lord and he repented. "My ears had heard of you, but now my eyes have seen you. Therefore I despise myself and repent in dust and ashes." Job 42:5-6. Then instead of Satan attacking him, God was blessing him with twice as much as he had before, including ten beautiful children. God's blessings have not diminished because His purpose for His people has always been the same since the creation. It is for us today. Read Galatians 3:14—"He redeemed us in order that the blessing given to Abraham might come on the Gentiles through Christ Jesus so that by faith we might receive the promise of the Spirit." This means that the way God blessed Abraham, his family, and the nation is the same for believers today.

Then God once again in Galatians 3:29 said, "If you belong to Christ, then you are Abraham's seed, and heirs according to the promise." It is so thrilling that God's creation purpose is still promised to His people today. Don't identify with the Job who sits on the ash heap with Satan in control, but with the Job who hears God's Word and responds to it.

Your victory is as certain as Job's. God knows Satan better than any one of us and God knows how Satan loves to attack us. God has not changed. What he did for Job, He will do for you. Saints, God is for you and wants you to have the victory.

Printed in the United States
By Bookmasters